Praise

A Baseball Family Album by Gene Carney grows out of the tradition of deftly expressed baseball commentaries by passionate and historically erudite fans of the sort that were once regularly available in *Fan*, a magazine edited by the late Mike Schacht.

Carney displays a fine knack for concisely distilling mixtures of fact and witty personal reflection to arrive at essential matters regarding great baseball players. He makes clever use of key phrases and events associated with his baseball men so that, by means of a sort of literary judo, the catch phrases and highlight moments for each player become the means to tell us who they really were. Because this is a "family album" his accounts of these baseball celebrities are generally presented as appreciations. Even when the personality traits or behaviors of these stars are problematical, Carney tends to remember them fondly as forgivable prodigal sons, ne'er-do-well brothers, and eccentric uncles within baseball's broad and complicated family. Let us, Carney suggests, remember with pleasure their foibles as much as their great feats. Though we are sometimes asked to forgive, little is forgotten. The misdeeds of a Ty Cobb or a Hal Chase are not glossed over and are acknowledged as important facets of who these guys were, but Carney wants us, first and foremost, to allow ourselves to rediscover and savor the history of the great game through recollection of the lives and characteristic performances of its best players.

The large number of pieces in Carney's collection – there are more than 130 – makes it a compendium of the entire history of the national pastime. The briskly alliterative and playfully colloquial phrasings by means of which Carney gives us his images can be flipped through in any order. He has provided us with an ample fistful of literary baseball cards.

-Joseph Stanton
Sport Literature Association

A Baseball Family Album

Gene Carney

Pocol Press

POCOL PRESS
Published in the United States of America
by Pocol Press
6023 Pocol Drive
Clifton, VA 20124
www.pocolpress.com

© 2008 by Gene Carney

All rights reserved. No part of this book may be reproduced in any form whatsoever without the express written consent of Pocol Press. Exceptions are made for brief quotations for criticism and reviews.

Publisher's Cataloguing-in-Publication

Carney, Gene 1946-

    A baseball family album / Gene Carney. – 1st ed. – Clifton, VA : Pocol Press, 2008.

    p. ; cm.

    ISBN: 978-1-929763-33-7

    1. Baseball player--Poetry. Baseball--Poetry. I. Title.

PS3553.A755 B37 2008
811.54–dc22   0803

Some of these poems first appeared in *Romancing the Horsehide*, McFarland, 1993.

ACKNOWLEDGEMENTS

I want to acknowledge first and most, the late Mike Schacht, whose *FAN Magazine* encouraged and inspired so many writers and readers. His editors, along with Mike, were extremely helpful in suggesting ways to make many of my poems (and short stories) more interesting to the eyes and ears.

Likewise, the editors of *Elysian Fields Quarterly*, *Spitball*, and other publications, some long gone like many of the people recalled in this book, for giving space to the few "baseball poets" who enrich our language. Once upon a time, poems appeared regularly on the sports pages and in columns, by Grantland Rice, Franklin P. ("Tinker to Evers to Chance") Adams, and many others. A few, like *Casey at the Bat*, became part of our culture. Baseball nicknames once added a lot of spice to baseball, too, and I hope they return someday, with the poetry.

Finally, a special thanks to Tom Hetrick and Pocol Press, for the opportunity to share this collection with you.

PREFACE

When I started writing baseball in 1989, I started with a book. I was advised that the book was OK, but would be a tough sell for a first-time author. And so I started building my resume, writing shorter stuff: articles, short stories, and dozens of little items that looked like poems.

With a little help from some editors who were not overly polite, these short "portraits" of ballplayers became poems, and found their way into literary baseball magazines, and a variety of newsletters and "fanzines" as they were called in the early 1990s. Virtually my first 125 baseball poems on players and the game were published by McFarland in 1993, under the title *Romancing the Horsehide*.

Some of the poems in *Romancing*, now out of print, are in this collection. But most of the portraits here have never been published before, except perhaps in my *Notes from the Shadows of Cooperstown*, begun in 1993 and moved to the internet in 1999 – you can look it up, as Casey Stengel would say, at www.baseball1.com/notes.

Most of the poems are a mix of research and imagination. For some, whole biographies or autobiographies were read, before I composed a line. That said, few of the poems were researched very deeply, and I'm almost certain that my friends in the Society for American Baseball Research (SABR) will delight in pointing out some fact or statistic that is either wrong or out of date. For example, in *Romancing*, pitcher Walter Johnson has 416 wins – that is now 417. Hack Wilson's RBI record, for decades thought to be 190, is now 191. But the statistics in this book are strictly secondary.

The leadoff poem really sets the tone for everything that follows. Baseball people are family, for better and for worse. Everyone in the family has their own favorites. Like many family albums, this will likely be a mix of familiar folks and some pretty obscure ones. This is not a Hall of Fame, where only high achievers gain entry. This is a *family* album, where everybody, saint and sinner, famous and unknown, are related.

I hope readers enjoy looking up their own favorites, and then learn more about those in the family whom they may not have ever met or even heard of. That's what albums are for, I think, to help us talk across the generations.

TABLE OF CONTENTS

A Baseball Family Album		1
Alexander[1]	Alexander Cartwright	2
Father	Henry Chadwick	3
Candy	Candy Cummings	4
Cap	Cap Anson	6
King	King Kelly	7
The Tall Tactician	Connie Mack	9
Kenesaw Mountain	Kenesaw Mountain Landis	11
Cy	Cy Young	12
Cousin Ed	Ed Barrow	13
The Old Fox	Clark Griffith	14
Ee-Yah	Hughie Jennings	15
The Hoosier Thunderbolt	Amos Rusie	16
Iron Man	Joe McGinnity	17
Wee Willie	Wee Willie Keeler	18
Little Napoleon	John McGraw	19
The Old Arbitrator	Bill Klem	20
The Flying Dutchman	Honus Wagner	21
Happy Jack	Jack Chesbro	22
Nap	Napoleon Lajoie	24
The Peerless Leader	Frank Chance	25
Three-Finger	Mordecai Brown	26
Rube	Rube Waddell	27
Germany	Germany Schaefer	28
Hooks	Hooks Wiltse	29
The Duke of Tralee	Roger Bresnahan	31
Addie	Addie Joss	32
Matty	Christy Mathewson	33
Wahoo Sam	Sam Crawford	34
The Legend of Faust	Charles Victor Faust	36
Big Ed Walsh	Ed Walsh	38
Gavvy	Gavvy Cravath	39
The Crab	Johnny Evers	40

---

[1] The names in this book appear in chronological order, according to date of birth.

The Mahatma	Branch Rickey	41
Big Ed Reulbach	Ed Reulbach	42
Prince Hal	Hal Chase	43
Chief	Chief Bender	44
Home Run	Frank Baker	45
Georgia Peach	Ty Cobb	46
Slap	Cy Slapnicka	47
Cocky	Eddie Collins	49
Harry	Harry Hooper	51
Low and Away	Grover Cleveland Alexander	52
Big Train	Walter Johnson	53
Bonehead	Fred Merkle	54
Hippo	Hippo Vaughn	56
The Grey Eagle	Tris Speaker	58
Shoeless Joe	Joe Jackson	59
Smoky Joe	Smoky Joe Wood	60
The Old Professor	Casey Stengel	61
Stuffy	Stuffy McInnis	62
Sub	Carl Mays	63
Honest	Eddie Murphy	64
Deacon	Everett Scott	65
Bullet Joe	Joe Bush	66
Sad Sam	Sam Jones	67
Ol' Stubblebeard	Burleigh Grimes	68
The Sizzler	George Sisler	69
Bambino	Babe Ruth	70
Rajah	Rogers Hornsby	71
Memphis Bill	Bill Terry	73
Pie	Pie Traynor	74
Gabby	Gabby Hartnett	75
Hack	Hack Wilson	76
Lefty	Lefty Grove	78
Bucketfoot Al	Al Simmons	79
Meal Ticket	Carl Hubbell	80
Mechanical Man	Charlie Gehringer	81
Cool Papa	Cool Papa Bell	82
Iron Horse	Lou Gehrig	84
Black Mike	Mickey Cochrane	85
Big Poison	Paul Waner	86

Pepper	Pepper Martin	87
The Lip	Leo Durocher	88
Brother Rick	Rick Ferrell	89
Satchel	Satchel Paige	90
Bill	Bill Dickey	91
Double X	Jimmie Foxx	92
Buck	Buck Leonard	93
Red	Red Barber	95
Billy	Billy Herman	96
Bucky	Bucky Walters	97
Master Melvin	Mel Ott	98
Smiling Stan	Stan Hack	99
Dizzy	Dizzy Dean	100
Hammerin' Hank	Hank Greenberg	101
Josh	Josh Gibson	102
Arky	Arky Vaughan	103
The Big Cat	Johnny Mize	104
As in Wreck	Bill Veeck	106
Yankee Clipper	Joe DiMaggio	108
Dutch Master	Johnny Vander Meer	109
Country	Enos Slaughter	111
Gunner	Bob Prince	112
The Mayor of Wrigley Field	Hank Sauer	114
Rapid Robert	Bob Feller	116
The Kid	Ted Williams	118
Jackie	Jackie Robinson	119
Pistol Pete	Pete Reiser	120
The Man	Stan Musial	121
Holy Cow!	Harry Caray	122
Prince Hal	Hal Newhouser	123
Campy	Roy Campanella	124
Spahnie	Warren Spahn	125
The Whip	Ewell Blackwell	126
Ralph	Ralph Kiner	127
Yogi	Yogi Berra	128
Harvey on the Mound	Harvey Haddix	129
The Duke	Duke Snider	131
Robin	Robin Roberts	132
Smoky	Smoky Burgess	133

Eddie	Eddie Mathews	134
Mr. Cub	Ernie Banks	136
Mickey	Mickey Mantle	137
Say Hey	Willie Mays	138
Rocky	Rocky Colavito	139
Mr. Tiger	Al Kaline	141
Hammer	Hank Aaron	143
Roberto	Roberto Clemente	144
Hoot	Bob Gibson	146
Frank	Frank Robinson	147
Sandy	Sandy Koufax	149
Maz	Bill Mazeroski	151
Hondo	Frank Howard	152
Brooksie	Brooks Robinson	154
The Dominican Dandy	Juan Marichal	156
Billy	Billy Williams	158
Stretch	Willie McCovey	159
Sixty-Nine	Ron Santo	161
Willie	Willie Stargell	163
Pete Rose	Pete Rose	165
Fergie	Ferguson Jenkins	167
Little Joe	Joe Morgan	168
Tom Terrific	Tom Seaver	170
Mr. October	Reggie Jackson	172
Johnny	Johnny Bench	174
Jim	Jim Rice	175
You Know Me, Don't You?		177

A BASEBALL FAMILY ALBUM

Without the iconic numbers --
Cy's 511, Ted's .406, the Babe's 60 --
Without the fabulous legends,
Tall tales of Josh's homers that land
In the next city on the next day,
Without the headlines and box scores,
They are still there.

We recognize their faces
From black-and-white photos
And newsreels and pieces
Of cardboard that sold tobacco.
Their trademark stances, windups and deliveries,
Slings and swings, trots around the sacks,
Head-first slides home....

They have become family.
Sometimes we know their nicknames
Best of all --
No one is anonymous
And each has left something behind,
Not just the tools of their craft:
Horsehide and leather,
White ash and muddy metal cleats,
Pinstriped jerseys and wire-rimmed sun glasses;
Not just trophies and rings and the stuff
Of attic trunks and gameroom displays.

We have memories:
Stories told between generations,
Embellished over hot stoves,
Recalled every summer
In the grandstand and bleachers
When something out there jogs
Something in here
Where they will live
As long as the Game
Is played.

ALEXANDER

Giving credit where it's due
Isn't always easy --
Ask Alexander Joy Cartwright
(Or Daniel Lucius Adams)

A Cooperstown plaque
Credits Cartwright --
Standout of the game's first team photo --
With three sublime assists:

Setting the bases
Ninety feet apart:
Stretching the child's game
Into adulthood

Setting nine innings
As the timepiece:
Not the tallies, not the minutes
Just nine for time

Setting nine players
As the team:
Nine to defend the fair field
Nine to rotate at the bat
Best nine against nine

Lots of folks say
"One of these days
We've got to get organized" --
But Cartwright (& Co.) *did* it

Yet the game's paternity
Remains cloudy --
What seems certain
Fittingly enough
Is that it was a team effort
Probably the work of at least
Nine

FATHER

Teenage immigrant
From the land of rounders
Henry caught the New York strain
Of the national virus
Soon to be pastime

The seedling sport
Was without foliage
When this son of a journalist
Came along to tend
Its all-American growth

His pen swatted away
Its pesky attackers
As his prose nurtured,
Like gentle sunlight, its rooting
And its climb heavenward

Editor of guides, chronicler of rule books
He watched and weeded, wrote and seeded
Cultivated the shape of the game
Taught it language

Perhaps his sense of
The beauty and wonder in each contest
Was behind his skepticism of
Homers and championship games:
Let runs be earned by hits and wits
Let no inning be called meaningless

His name was penciled in
The Elysian Fields lineup
But his work was all outside the lines
Recall that name when marvelling
At the economy of the box score
The same name bronzed
In Cooperstown's Hall:
Henry Chadwick

CANDY

Doesn't really matter
If he did or didn't
Invent the curveball
Any more than if Abner
Invented the game
Some folks will think it's important
To give some rugged individual American
All the credit
But most are content to
Behold the beauty

William Arthur Cummings
Said he received the heavenly vision
While tossing clam shells on the beach
Years of practice with a sphere
Before others saw the miracle

Throwing underhand
Kid gloves on the pitching hand
With a snap of his wrist
Mad scientist breathed life
Into the ball that had been dead
"It's alive!" shrieked the villagers
And the secret monster curve
Claimed its helpless first victims

No refuge from this arc
No escaping the captain's hook
No convincing the physics skeptics
No forgiveness from the batsmen
Candy threw it best
Until it took its toll on his arm
Pain took over for the starter Joy
Finishing Cummings' game

Columbus discovered America:
Never mind that he found people here
Doubleday invented baseball:
Pay no attention

To the family resemblance
To Rounders or One Old Cat
Or to the Knickerbocker game
Of Alexander Joy Cartwright

And Candy Cummings fathered the curve:
Fred Goldsmith and the others
Doomed to oblivion
While Candy is in Cooperstown with --
Cartwright!
History throws curves, too!

CAP

Superstar when the NL was hatched
First to lead a team to a pennant
Adrian Anson played hardball
Nineteen sparkling 19th century summers
Earning his epitaph:
Here lies a man who batted .300

Pioneer of spring training
Precision drillmaster
Innovative strategist when
Argumentative captain at the helm
First to three thousand hits
This Ballplayer's Career
Capped long after he was gone:
Hall

Too bad he was so good a player
Because when he drew the color line
With his intimidating siren voice
Actor strutting the dusty stage
July 20, 1884
People listened
For over six decades
So that today Jackie Robinson
Is a household name
While Moses Fleetwood Walker
Answers tough trivia

No doubt if Cap hadn't spoken up
Someone else would have
Majority rules
And the times, they weren't a changin'

All we can say for sure
Is that Cap Anson had the chance
To be a far different kind of hero
Maybe history will prove
We all do

KING

Wore the diamond's crown
When the kingdom was brand new
Its subjects relatively few
But fervent

A generation before the Babe
Michael Joseph Kelly was
Baseball's matinee idol
Immortalized in song
King Kelly did a Chicago
Hook slide
Into America's hearts --
Daring young man
On the flying spikes
Boldly diving head-first
For bases and adulation

Traded for a record
Five-digit figure
(Where will it all end?)
Kelly's fans boycotted in protest
Except when his new team was in town

King Kelly had a flair
For the game and fine clothes
Leader in color no matter what league
Irishman batted and fielded his teams
To an octet of pennants

The King was dead
Soon after leaving the Game
But sightings persist:
Who scored six runs?
Who stole six bases?
Who stole the camera by wearing
His insides outside
For even the umpires to see?
Who's the flamboyant fellow
Cutting corners

Thinking around the rules
Revving up the crowd
Filling up the stadium?

Sight the King
Every time you see a line form
For autographs
Every time a player is paid
Entertainer's wages
By the high bidder
Long live the King

THE TALL TACTICIAN

While the fans bought scorecards
To tell the players
Connie Mack used his
To set his fielders on defense

For fifty years
Irishman born Cornelius McGillicuddy
Perched on dugout bench
Savvy businessman manager
Wearing suit and tie
Long-sleeved shirts with collars
Even on the hottest days
Polished unspiked shoes
And the grim visage of war

Connie Mack endured at the helm
Because it was his ship
And he loved sailing

Great grandfather rock
Of the Phiiadelphia A's
Emperor of dynasties
Long-suffering saint
Of the lesser teams
When his stars were too expensive
For his modest galaxy
Mack became the patriarch
Not just of his team or league
But of the sport itself

Lots of Connie Mack
Rubbed off on the game
Over the time of his life:
Dignity and respect
Move up the ladder by
Honest hard work

Grand old man was still at it
Thirteen years after
His plaque went up in the Hall
Proof that the baseball can be
A fountain of youth --
Mr. Mack was Methuselah
Somehow outwitting the hourglass
Until immortality was just
A short sacrifice bunt away

KENESAW MOUNTAIN

Carved from granite
Named for a Civil War battle site
Landis entered the Game
Looking for the save
Dusting off all
Who would dig in against him
And dominating

When the black sox were burned
White smoke rose
Signalling the beginning
Of his pontifical reign

His terrible swift decisions
Were meted out with iron fists
And without mercy
Given absolute power to act on
Despite the caveat of Acton
The judge did without courts of appeal
Which might have offset
His all too human justice

Craggy countenance
Grim glare like a bird of prey
Below the silver crown
Struck those prone to bribe and gamble
With fear and trembling
His steely words ended careers
Benched even the Babe
Even as they restored confidence
If not integrity

Since the Czar stepped down
Twenty-some summers of
Giving not an inch
Over at last, other Commissioners have ruled
But none quite like Judge Landis
For better and worse

CY

How ya gonna keep the boy from Ohio
Down on the farm
With an arm like *that*?

Cleveland's Spiderman
Lightning spinnings tied up his prey
Mismatched
Their sticks
Against his fog

Colossus of country roads
Winning ball games was as ordinary for Cy
As doing the chores
Pitching hay or nickel curves
Breaking bats or topsoil
Warming up wastes sunlight
Do what you're there to do
Pursue the outs one at a time
Excellence found in the unhurried pace
No need to think about it much
Once it's become routine

Maybe in his case
A single number *is* a fair description:
511
When it came to winning
Nobody did it better
Won twenty in his off-seasons
Thirty or more, five times
But never got the Award
Didn't need any blue ribbons
Save them for the livestock at the fair
Denton True *was*
Cy Young

COUSIN ED

Never played the game
But he left his mark
Sure as the signature
Of Honus Wagner on a pro contract
Or Ruth in the lineup
On the days he wasn't pitching

Ed Barrow was a force
To be reckoned with
Whether manager or exec --
Locomotive on track
Engine a'steaming
Without a brakeman
Collision course set for October

First tasted ultimate ecstasy
At Boston's helm
Winning the shortened race in '18
When the Bambino was
But an Adolescent Sultan

Abandon ship:
Followed the Babe to NY

For two dozen dynastic summers
Barrow tended the farms
Traded for pennant-race horses
And plugged Yankee cashbox leaks --
Turned out Ed
Was Cousin to success

THE OLD FOX

Young Griff knew the sweet pain
Of the starting pitcher,
Right arm drained 300 innings
In Chicago summers
Brush strokes painting twenty wins.
Old Griff taught the strategy
Of the reliever
Proving fresh pen men mightier.

Young Griff knew the pocketbook pain
Of the player under contract,
And threw different kinds of strikes
At Scroogey opponents.
Old Griff became an owner himself,
After managing to midwife
Ban Johnson's American League --
Kept the fans entertained
With another Johnson,
Riding the Big Train to the top.

The General was unstubborn:
Supporting the prohibition
Of the scuffers and spitballs
That once resided in his arsenal,
Serving up night games
That he once doubted,
Finding a nest for the Goose
That he once could not afford.

Like Connie Mack
Clark gave so much to the Game
For so long
That it seemed natural
To name a ballpark
Griffith Stadium.

EE-YAH

Carved from Pennsylvania anthracite
Hughie Jennings roared into baseball
Brawling old Orioles' captain --
Shortstop hustled hits and pennants
Hustled around the rules
With a lawyer's talent
For strategy and tactics

It was Hughie's great fortune
To hold that Tiger Cobb
In the hand Detroit dealt him:
Three straight flags
Started his long reign
As manager and coach

Jennings turned the box
Outside the lines at third base
Into a conductor's podium:
Fortissimo cheerleading
Allegro on the bases
Never *sotto voce* or *largo*

Photographers have frozen him:
Jennings forever perches
On a single limb
Hands eternally clapping or flapping
Mouth open but silent:
Yet we hear echoing over the years
Guided missiles and whistles
Taunting and haunting
Keeping the rally alive:
Eeeee-YAHHH!

THE HOOSIER THUNDERBOLT

Might better have been tagged
Shooting Star:
Amos Rusie lit up the dead-ball sky
Decade before the century turned
And the famous Amos arm
Burned out

Farmer grew to size
As an iron Giant in the city
That magnifies:
Zeus hurling imprecise lightning
Crackling wild with K's
Five hundred innings a summer
Harvesting W's in sunny fields

Sat out one of those seasons
Refusing to throw a knuckler
In a salary dispute:
Might have changed the game
Even more
But he settled for his due
Instead of the reserve clause

Imagine Nolan Ryan
Ten feet closer to home
Allowed to work from a box
Released from the rubber:
Not hard to understand why
Catcher fortified his mitt with lead
And why Amos Wilson Rusie
Usually stood tall and victorious
At the end of the ninth

Batters couldn't stand the heat
So they made the *mound* retreat
To its present sixty feet
Six inches

IRON MAN

Young Joe McGinnity worked in a foundry
So he had that nickname long before
His rookie season at age twenty-eight
Older Joe M. simply gave the phrase
A whole new meaning

Give him the ball
And you might not get it back
Stay out there all day
Both ends of the doubleheader
Finishes starts
For himself or others

Little Napoleon had it easy
Selecting his weapons:
Give the other soldiers a rest
Give the ball to the Iron Man
Let him toss Old Sal to Bresnahan
Come back tomorrow with Mathewson

Roundhouse nickel rockets
Launched from the side
Dead ball from live arm
The Iron Man cometh
Days without end

Compliment to Christy
Old Oriole like McGraw
Giant workload hauled
Over just ten ML summers
But kept pitching till fifty-four:
McGinnity's arm at rest at last
Just a few years before
The Iron Man himself
Surrendered

Perhaps life without Old Sal
Too lonely to bear

WEE WILLIE

Sometimes plain answers
Turn out to be the most memorable:
Rob banks because that's where money is
Bat over .400 by hitting the ball
Where they ain't

Five-four-and-a-half rookie Giant
Nothing small about outfielder
William Henry Keeler's deeds
Over nearly two score seasons:
Flying number two slot for the old Orioles
Hit the ground swinging in Brooklyn
Then in pinstripes across town --
Hit nearly three thousand
Where they ain't

Paired with the slightly taller
Fellow New Yorker quick raw McGraw
As partners in hit-and-run crime
Masters of the Baltimore chop
Well-placed lethal bunts
And one-two punch hits --
McGraw led off with temper
Willie followed with the temperament
Of a more cheerful aggression
Inside Ned Hanlon's baseball

Hero for all little people
Wee Willie showed that size
Mattered less than savvy
Bat control and speed down the line

No doubt Willie was jockeyed
By those who mistook his height
For his real magnitude
Of course today Keeler
Is in the sport's Hall of Fame
Where they ain't

LITTLE NAPOLEON

John McGraw
Fundamentalist before the
Fundamentals got around
Baseball's answer to Franklin and Edison
Old Oriole invented new ways to win
Every time his team took the field

So much of baseball's family
Bears a strong resemblance
To this patriarch of the inside game
His genes dominant as his Giants
In the scrappy skippers who fight
Tooth and nail for their players
And their victories
Anything goes
For the generals at war

The game has his eyes
Nothing escaped them
No opportunity for the extra base or run
No chance to cut down the enemy rally
Or slow the enemy runner
No occasion to instruct
Motivate
Lead

Eyes lit by fire
Eyes for talent buried in
Sons of miners and farmers
Eyes for intimidating
Authorities upstairs or between the lines
And all those not on his side
Eyes for the advantage everywhere
His armies hit and ran
Like Colonial soldiers
Disciplined by a tyrant
Tactics was Mr. McGraw's
Business

THE OLD ARBITRATOR

Klem was the rock
Upon which was built
Respect
For the law and the order
Umps enforce
To make possible
Play

To be labeled "Fair":
Is there a greater compliment
To seek
In any profession?

The lines he drew
In the dust of diamonds
No doubt infuriated those who knew
The step across
Put them in the showers

The lines set boundaries
As Bill's manner
Set patterns
For generations
Of men in black

"Never missed one"
Proclaimed the authority
"In my heart"
Added the man

Besides the calls of
Fair or foul
Strike or ball
Bill Klem
Took his games
Safely out of dispute
And made the fields
Even

THE FLYING DUTCHMAN

Is there a greater irony
Than that Sweet Caporal tobacco card
Selling in today's marketplace
For more than twice the Dutchman ever earned
In his radiant score of seasons?

Its unimaginable value the result
Of Honus' contempt
For opportunistic bucks

Hans just said No
To those who would buy his soul
Disdain
As rare then as now

Triple threat
He manufactured victories
With his tools of wood and leather
His bow-legged base-to-base swiftness
And play
Hard as the spikes
That carried him home

How fitting it is the face of Wagner --
The Pirate who loved the game so much
That he'd have suited up for nothing --
Even on that cardboard scrap
He gazes with clear conscience
His life and livelihood uncompromised
A snapshot from the less-traveled road

HAPPY JACK

Armed with damp deliveries
John Dwight Chesbro
Was cream
Rising only slowly
To the top of his craft

Pitched the Pirates to two flags
But jumped to the Highlanders
Missing the first World Series

Came close again next year
Forty-one wins
Forty-eight complete games
But Jack was not happy in the end:
Standing on that peak
Chesbro uncorked a wild pitch
Letting in a pennant-clinching
Bosox run

Fickle fate
That would lift a man to heights
Then let him fall:
Why do we remember the two
As if they were equal

Climb of half a year
Half a hundred and more times
Of taking the mound
Getting enemy batters out
One at a time
Over thirteen hundred times
In the pinches
In the heat and rain
In the pressure of a race

Suddenly a pitch slips
It rises
Missile out of control
No way to abort

To yank back or cancel
Undo the pitch sailing
Past the backstop's head
As the runner from third
Breaks home
Slides through the crack
His team on top for good now

Jack's happiness was in the climb
His humanity in that final throw

NAP

Never played in a Series
Denied the national light of October
That might have linked his name
With some great catch or smash
Made it household

What survives of his time in the game
Besides his numbers
Is that marvelous name

Whole afternoons can be spent
Arguing how to pronounce it
Not Napoleon of course
But the other part

And Lajoie turns up all over:
Lists of your average kings
Keystone wizards
Dynamic doublers
The 3M Club
The Hall

Sooner or later
You had to pitch to him
Sooner or later
We need to learn how
To say his name right
If we want to talk baseball

THE PEERLESS LEADER

Pharaoh of the Cub Dynasty
That followed right after
The century turned
Into baseball's Modern Times,
Frank Chance
Four times
Reached the pyramid's peak

Not by chance
Did his teams
Win two of every three
(And *116* once upon a time!) --
First was where he played
First was where he aimed

Needed no Adams' poem
To make his mark
In the game's lexicon:
Did it with iron-fisted
Motivation --
"Husk" led by example,
One (stolen) base at a time

Chance to Tinker
(Evers covering first
On the sacrifice bunt try)
Was the stratagem that
Made this trio feared:
What they *did,*
Not the ditty

Frank had the chances
In his day
To better the best:
McGraw and Cobb

And he did

THREE-FINGER

The seventh summer
Of any boy's life
Can be an awakening of sorts
Join the gang
Try your hand at new sports
For Mordecai Peter Centennial Brown
It was clearly a turning point
Thanks to his uncle's corn-cutter:
Took his fingers
Gave him an arsenal

Ace of the Cubbie dynasty
He hurled like he wanted
To stay out of the coal mines
Job he had before this one

Take a time-machine ride back
To see the craftsman Brown at work
Chances are
Matty's on the hill for the Giants
Three-Finger and Christy
Batters beware
Sure better play for one run today
Goose eggs in the air
Sudden death from the first pitch
Mordecai hurled like he knew the cost
Of one mistake
In any inning of life

RUBE

Not sure if every flake is unique
But this one sure was

Southpaw strikeout artist
With heat comparable to Walter's
George Edward Waddell
Controlled the game from the hill --
Trouble was, he'd rather be fishing

How eccentric was Rube?
Roommate insisted that Rube's contract
Contain a no-crackers-in-bed clause --
That pledge he could keep

Chasing fire engines or leading parades
Serving up or quaffing down drinks --
Don't count on Waddell to mind P's & Q's
But when he was out there on the mound
K's and W's were dependable

First to whiff three hundred a season
Sixteen in a game
And the side on nine pitches --
Made misnomers of contact hitters

Probably enjoyed exhibition games more --
Could give his fielders a rest
As the only player on the field
Struck out the side

Baseball gave Rube a focus
But could not focus on Rube:
Too eccentric for definition
Never knew what was in his head
Judge this talent rather by his arm
Unlucky in love and money
Rube was the comic page in color
Somehow stuck in the sports section

GERMANY

Stole first -- or did he?
Since the rule changed
No one else ever will.

Stole first
After he stole second --
Dusting himself off
Herman Schaefer scowled
Because third was *still*
Occupied by the winning run.

So Germany stole first:
Not to pad his stats
But to set up the replay --
And to be sure it worked,
He shouted to his teammate
Leading off third
That he was going again.

This time the catcher threw
And missed, and that was the game.

Germany Schaefer was zany
By all accounts,
But stealing first was brainy.
(Of course if he'd have been nailed going back
We might judge differently!)

Antics between the lines
Continued when he stood outside,
Clowning with Altrock
And then on the vaudeville stage.

Say what you will about Germany,
He got something right:
Baseball entertains folks
And ought to be fun
For everyone in the park.

HOOKS

For a while,
It looked like no opposing navy could sink
George Wiltse
As he reeled off twelve straight W's
Before getting snagged with an L.

Upstate fingerling took the bait,
Was scooped up on the great
McGraw destroyer.

Judge this fish
By the school in which
His career numbers swim:
Above forty-some 'Famers
In the 60-percent victory boat,
Above thirty-some
In stifling opposition oars,
And in keeping the infield ports clear.

Off to see the world --
A World bigger than a Series.
Eclipsed by the bigger fish --
Mathewson, McGinnity, Marquard --
Hooks lurked in deeper waters,
Only breaking the surface a few times:
Shining leap, 7 K in two (sp)innings;
Saving a big game win for Big Six
With first-base nettings;
Pulling Philly hitless into the tenth
While yielding only a single nibble,
Flashing his own holiday fireworks in '08:
Close to perfection, *but no cigar*
Except ever after from the angler in blue
Who let that strike wiggle off the hook.

Hooks was a Master and Commander
Of the realm of baseball,
His licorice-stained left hand

Kept his team's rudder
Bound for October's Game.
Like the *Old Man and the Sea*,
Completed his voyage
With unsung dignity,
A hero on the shores where he lived
When he wasn't sailing through history.

THE DUKE OF TRALEE

This Roger was not jolly
Nor did he fit the mold
For backstops:
Bresnahan was a McGraw Irishman
Who could play any position
For any team who could stand
His heat:
Those who couldn't did well
To stay in the kitchen

As rough on teammates and umpires
Owners and league officials
As on opponents
Roger broke in as a pitcher
But is known for his electricity
On the other end of the battery:
Stormy game-caller with
Lightning thinking and
Thunderous throws

Feisty lead-off hitter with speed
Bresnahan was behind the plate
Four Series shutouts in '05
(Matty's trio of gems
One more by the Iron Man) --
Made good his single chance
In the October sun

Credited with adding shin guards
And padding for wire masks
To the catchers' armor --
And helping the tools gain respect --
Roger was not known
For making things easier:
Fighter concentrating skills
On winning baseball games
As if they were prizes
Awarded to the last man standing

ADDIE

His sudden death just after Opening Day 1911
When hearts were filled with sheer hope
Jolted the sport

Addie Joss after all had a reputation
For finishing what he started
Cleveland's consummate starter
Nine times out of ten
When the day's battlesmoke cleared
Was still there

Addie Joss after all was a professional
It was his job to entertain
Those who worked in dingy factories
Or on Great Lakes barges
He took his vocation as seriously as they
So how could he not report to work this season?

Addie Joss after all was mortal
Despite his superhuman ERA
Transcendent collection
Of shutouts, no-hitters, and
Less quantifiable gems
And above all the respect
Earned from his peers

Perhaps if he'd have played longer
Eighteen or twenty summers
Instead of nine
Perhaps he'd have made more enemies
Familiarity with Addie Joss
Bred no contempt
His passing on early
Was celebrated by his leaguemates
With an impromptu All-star game
Proceeds to his widow
The perfect wake
Weep for joy

MATTY

Matty made his opponents talk to themselves:
"What's a college boy doin' in the game
Playin' with a bunch a red-neck ruffians
Who smoke n' drink n' raise hell off the field
Sundays too when
McGraw's right-hand man won't even pitch?
Pert' soon the ladies will want t' come 'n watch
Athletes don't write no books neither
Stick wit' the checkers and bridge, Bible-toter!

"Shoot the Giant don't walk nobody
Ain't no way t' touch them damn fade-aways
Ninth inning alrea --
Shut out agai --"

Matty brought to the marriage
Just what the spouse needed
Respectability
Gave his game something to shoot for
Then and tomorrow

Take away all the glittering digits
Even the Series of zeroes
They are but shadows
Of his thoughtful artistry
Mathewson stands tall without them
In control
Spell class act
Christy

WAHOO SAM

Nebraskan was born there --
By the time he retired
Town might claim to be named after
Sam Crawford --
Not the other way around

If the three-bagger
Is baseball's most exciting play
Then no one electrified the sport
As often as Sam --
Career homer record long smashed,
The tower of triples he built
Yet stands tallest in the sport

It endures like the memories
Of Crawford and Cobb --
Genial giant from the midwest
Batting behind the southern wildcat:
Dominating Detroit outfielders
Turning walks with Ty on third
Into double steals --
Turning pitches into hits
Hits into runs and runs
Into pennants

Crawford was the mass-murderer
Of the dead ball:
Weapon: heavy wooden club --
Leaves distinctive mark on its victims.
Scene of the crimes: the ballpark
Wherever Sam played was Murder City.
Motive: seemed to take great pleasure
In knocking his prey senseless
Giving them a ride
Burying them deep

When the game was tactics
Sam was the Cornhusker
Popping home the Cobb:

Sizzle followed by small explosions
Treats for fans in the stands
Enjoying the show,
Watching thinking men
Do

THE LEGEND OF FAUST

Charlie began his public life
At thirty in 1911 New York
Sure wasn't Kansas any more

Was it Mephistopheles
Or a fortune-teller
Who sent the message to McGraw:
If Charlie pitched
The Giants would win

Simple enough to test:
McGraw watched his windmill windup
Then started catching bare-handed
And started to wonder --
Saw *some*thing that day
No one else could see

Charles Victor Faust
Became part of the team
Warmed up every day
Thinking he was going to pitch --
Never got to the mound
But McGraw's Giants
Won the pennant

Next year, and a third time
Charm held like a witch's spell

Took a break to go on stage
Drawing card on Broadway
As at the Polo Grounds --
Giants lost four straight
Till Charlie returned
To break the streak:
His Giants needed him

Charlie's health failed in '14
McGraw finished second --

Faithful Charlie departed in '15
Giants finished dead last
Victory Faust gave baseball
Lots more than three summers
Of windmilling on the sidelines
And two real innings pitched:
Gave fans something to talk about
Think about --
Wonder years
About the soul of Faust

BIG ED WALSH

Wasn't called Big 'cause his son
Also pitched for the Chisox
Or 'cause he was some alpine hulk
Firing country sinkers from a mound
He didn't really need

Nope -- Call Ed Walsh
Who "could strut while standing still"
Big
For the wins he piled high
Mostly in seven dazzling middle seasons
With a handsome ERA over his career
That no one before or since has matched

(Or call him Big for the size of the outfield
The pitcher had a hand in designing
Old Comiskey Park!)

Big Ed came alive when the Hitless Wonders
Won it all in '06
Didn't need much with Walsh out there
Spitting K's and spinning 0's
Overhead and sidearm blurs
Dead balls pronounced strikes on arrival

The man who once worked coal
Turned to iron in '08
Big Iron: tons of innings
Two score wins and still
A trademark featherweight ERA

Ed Walsh's life entwined with perfection:
Joss had to be perfect to edge him 1-0
October 2 in that paragon summer --
Chicago's workhorse tossed some no-no's himself:
One in 1907 on May 26
Exactly 52 years before Haddix' perfect loss
And the loss to the world of Big Ed

GAVVY

If only the ball
Had stayed dead
Or the Babe a hurler
Then maybe his name today
Would be more familiar

Clifford Carlton Cravath
Cactus man from the old west
Home Run King of his day
Clouting nineteen twice
Before that marvelous
Summer of 1915
When the Phillie outfielder hit so many
That they thought the record would last forever:
Two dozen!

Gavvy led the league
Three more times after that
But never mustered more than twelve
As if the feat of climbing the peak
Had taken his best

But sure as The City of Brotherly Love
Was eclipsed by the
One That Doesn't Sleep
Gavvy's pyramid of twenty-four stones
Was soon dwarfed by Ruth's skyscrapers
Twenty-nine
Then *fifty*-nine stories tall

Gavvy's years out of the game
Must have been full of wonder:
Wonder how his thunder
Might have sounded
Against horsehide fresh
White and dry
Holding jackrabbit
Itching for a long ride

THE CRAB

Trojan at the Cub keystone
Middleman in the Adams poem as
Chance would have it
No reason to
Tinker with the lineup
Evers was the plotting manager's
Choice to lead the way to
October's game

Johnny was on the spot in '08
When Merkle made his infamous
Giant boner --
"Touch all the bases"
Credit Evers with an assist
On the cliche

Give him another A
For the Miracle in Boston
Pulled with the Rabbit
Out of the basement hat

In shallow or deep
Hard-shelled combatant
Inventor of strategy
As rough on those in blue
As on the invaders of his sack
Eye on the horsehide
As well as the cleat
Thinker Evers
Really left little to
Chance

THE MAHATMA

Mr. Rickey's nickname
Suggests a wise man
With a great soul
And prestige
Yet it sounds foreign

And perhaps he was
From a different world
From the future

A world where the Game
Thrived on talent
Mined by sharp eyes
And then raised on farms
To be harvested for
The tops of the pyramids

A world where the Game
Demanded spring rehearsals
Where mechanical arms
Tossed tirelessly to helmeted men
Inside cages

A world where the Game
Was played color blind
No Jackie needed
To make the teams reflect
The human rainbow
Of their cities and towns

Shrewd bow-tied lawyer
Branch Rickey
Puffed about the Game
Clouds of cigar smoke
And when they cleared
The Game had changed
Its very soul becoming
A little greater

BIG ED REULBACH

This Ed was big on wins:
109 his first six summers
While his Cubs took four flags
And two World Series
Reulbach helped them *rule*

Catchers dabbed their mitts
With white paint --
Ed Reulbach knew the real target
Was October's Game

Witness September 26, 1908:
In the heat of the plight
Big Ed gave his teammates' arms
The day off --
Tossing twin shutouts
Two giant steps forward
Toward the finish line
Tape and Giants broken in playoff

With two more fingers
Than his famous ace partner
Had a hand
In the first Series sweep

The Big Ed across town
Gained more fame as an ace --
Ed Reulbach was merely a king
Who enjoyed giving Cub fans
The royal flush
Of victory

PRINCE HAL

Hal Chase
Had reputations

One was that of the best-fielding
First-baseman of his day
Maybe any day:
Played it like a shortstop
Schooled in ballet and archery

Made plenty of errors though
How many intentional?

Another reputation
Was that he threw games
As easily as horsehides

Hal chased easy money
Hopping from team to team
One step ahead of accusing managers
Or the emerging long arm of law
Till finally he was put out
For life

Prince with red head crowned
In popularity
Hal Chase learned too late
Monogamy is required of ball players
By the nature of the sport
Divorce the penalty
For playing the field
Outside the lines

CHIEF

Charley Bender was no Sockalexis
Cleveland's original Indian
And a hard act to follow
But he was proud
Of his Chippewa heritage
Without reservation

Before he was twenty
He was in the A's rotation
With Plank and Waddell
Then in the first Mack Dynasty
Became a Series regular

Bender drew plenty of praise
Cobb: "brainiest" pitcher faced
But forget the words
He pitched the must-win games
The ones on the way to pennants
Or up against Mathewson
Duels in the cool October sun

He was no Chief, of course
But on the mound
Clearly he was in charge
Hostilities toward his race
Reduced to the one-on-one
Between himself and the batter
Bender fit only the stereotype
Of the clutch winner

HOME RUN

Good thing J. Franklin
Played ball back then
Or he'd wear the tag
Dinger or Tater
Or Gopher!

This fabulous Baker boy
Could slug the dead ball all right
Though his summer peak was
The original Baker's Dozen
His decisive October pair
Against McGraw's M-Boys
Earned him the nickname
Right place and time
For the dubbing

Connie Mack's
Hot corner man
In the $100,000 Infield
(Four stars for
Pinch-hitter's wages --
Those were the days)
The speedster with sock
Wielded a three-and-a-quarter pounder
Sturdy ungiving spar
Not unlike the wagon tongues on
His quiet Maryland farm

Frank summered there twice
In his playing days:
Casualty in the Federal League War
And then to be with his dying wife
Home Run Baker knew when
To step back from the game
And choose the heavier
Burdens

GEORGIA PEACH

Like all kids
I was fascinated by dinosaurs:
No family visit to the museum
Was without its long pause in their Hall
Where the fiercest of all
Tyrannosaurus Rex
Towering over cowering crowds
Commanding fear and respect
Ruled

Like all kids, I was impressed by big numbers
And another Ty's stats towered
As tall over the sport
As that museum reptile's skeleton over me
Over all but the Babe

Later I learned
Ruth had won the hearts of all America
While Cobb won hardly a friend
As if his file-sharpened spikes
Had gashed the ankles of the nation
Who thought they were in it for fun

They said he played like a man possessed
And maybe this Georgian was
Haunted by his father's ghost
To excel at any cost
And it cost him dearly

I imagine the last tyrannosaurus
Facing extinction
Got little sympathy
From those once terrorized
Their scars reminders
That some breeds
Need to rule
Their own cruel league
At any cost

SLAP

Only pitched in ten games himself
Cyril Slapnicka of Cedar Rapids
Is remembered best
For his eye

Not his batting eye:
Cy was a scout --
Had to see the man in the boy
Sift talent and sign it up

Had an eye not for legs
But for arms:
For over three decades
Cleveland managers were
Slap-happy with his ivory:
Hudlin and Harder
Feller and Score

Wheeler and dealer
Cy's contracts often rated
Invitations to see the Judge --
Commissioner Landis, that is
Usually got his targets:
Dollar day bargain Feller
(Toss in the autographed ball)
Or booming bonuses for the babies

Long before radar guns
Slap had a nose for speed
That would endure
And ripen into ML strikes

Mind-reader had X-ray vision
To see the invisible stuff within
Prospects' performances
To probe hearts and stomachs
Using instincts developed on his own
With the poise of a gambler

Imagine Cy the day
He caught his first glimpse
Of the sixteen-year-old kid
Firing Iowa smoke --
For minutes or hours
Cy's imagination rushing ahead
Sees the uniform change and
Hears the cheers multiply --
When the final out
Rudely ends his trance
Cy wakes and starts making
Someone else's dream come true

COCKY

Of all the Collins who played the game
None played longer or better or bolder
Than Eddie

Quarter of a century at the keystone
Sparkplug of the A's early dynasty
Later kept his own ChiSox White
Collins oozed with confidence
Hit-and-run driver of teams
And self

Owner of position four in the scorebook
His career is summed up in threes:
Three-thirty-three batter
With thirty-three hundred hits
And three ways to win:
Wood, leather or brain
Collins stole signals
Like he stole bases
And the show

Fans looked for Eddie's gum
Stuck on his cap's button when he stood
Square in the batter's box
Until he had two strikes
Then the gum and Eddie's brain
Went to work
Putting the pitcher
In bubble trouble

Pencil in Eddie Collins at second
On the All-October team
Chances are good he'll get on
Speed around the bases
Maybe score the key run
In the final game:
He was that kind of guy

How fitting that our last image

Comes from a picture taken
At the sport's new shrine:
Beside the Babe and Mr. Mack
Speedster sits at rest
Hands folded
Comfortable with greatness
Probably chewing gum
And stealing
The photographer's signals

HARRY

Mr. Hooper signed on with the Red Sox
Hoping to engineer the new Fenway
Instead
Stayed twelve summers in right field
Top of the line-up
Dash for triples and pilfers
Harry completed the Million Dollar trio
Of the Boston dynasty

Harry's lethal right arm
Was a concealed automatic weapon
Gattling gun spraying assists
Mowing and cowing down runners

Harry also had a famous rump
On which he slid to snag flies
Or block hits his way --
And a golden bare right hand
That snagged at once Doyle's smash
And a Series win in 1912

Four Octobers
Ended for Harry Hooper
With top-of-the-world celebrating

But of all his assists
Perhaps the greatest
Was his convincing Manager Barrow
To try the young southpaw
Between starts
In the outfield --
See if it helps the game having more
Of Babe Ruth

LOW AND AWAY

When Alexander joined in
The civil war
Between pitcher and hitter
That broke out loud when
He was growing up
Pete was Ulysses --
S. Grant, that is
Battling on several fronts
The batters were easier to master
Than the alcohol and
The prohibitionist managements

Pete's work on the diamond
Spoke louder than he --
His solitariness
An asset on the mound
When it was one on one
When a strike or shutout was needed
Pete delivered

In all the seasons between
His brilliant break-in rookie
And his inglorious clinging struggle
At the end
The war raged on all fronts

Epilepsy confused with intemperance
Pete half-listened to or half-heard
Those outside the lines where he battled

Looking back we see double:
Always that image
Of the single Series save
The four clutch pitches to Lazzeri
Superimposed over two decades of deeds
Not likely to be seen again
Achieved one day at a time
The innings when Pete was in control

BIG TRAIN

If there are zeroes on the scoreboard
And smoke between the mound and the batter's box
Walter's probably out there tossing
His speed

Pity the poor backstop
His hands punished by the thuds
Velocity that radar guns
Could only dream about tracking

While his Senators filibustered runs
The Big Train smashed home
Clearing batsmen off the rails
Pounding like ocean waves on boulders
As awesome a sight as a coastal storm
A feast of wind and sound

The Big Train smashed home
Carving over the years a grand canyon
Making forever marks on the face of the game
Five score and ten shutouts
A pile of W's 417 high
And an upper-deck row of K's
That stretch from the Capitol to Cooperstown
Johnson was the other
Washington Monument

BONEHEAD

The kid was nineteen and fifty games
Into his career when it happened

Umpires' worst nightmare:
Polo Grounds awash in jubilant fans
Home team having edged the Cubs
In a game reeking of October
Winning run jogged home
After the heroic two-out
Tie-breaking single in the ninth
Nothing left to do
If you're the runner on first
But touch second and run for cover

Fred Merkle ran first
And from then on
Could never hide
The post-mortem force play
Forcing more post-season play and
Sudden death for the Giants

To blunder is human
And to lay blame
The divine right of scribes
Merkle's misfortune was to have erred
In the spotlight of center stage
And while others have muffed lines
Or stumbled over props
Fred's performance got a one-word review
That stuck like tarpaper

And it wasn't "scapegoat"
But it could've been

To his credit
Frederick Charles Merkle
Went on to touch (and steal) thousands of bases
En route to five World Series
The kid made good despite the cruel tag

Succeeded despite being voted least likely
And today is listed in Macmillan's
With no nickname at all
Forgiven

HIPPO

Was big
But he ran like one --
That's why the nickname
For James Leslie

Cub with a sub-
Lime ERA
Hippo Vaughn
Galumphed to twenty wins regularly
And once pulled his team
To the Series

Poor Hippo
That 1918 post-season
Of a short-season:
Gave up five singles and lost
1-0 to Babe Ruth's Bosox
When his Cubs finally scored
For Hippo
One wasn't enough:
2-1 loss to Carl Mays

On two days rest Hippo
Took the hill again
Pitched a shutout
Just to be safe

That wasn't the first
Hippodrome tragedy:
Second of May the season before
Hippo held the Reds hitless
But his Cubs managed exactly that many
Off his dueling partner Fred Toney
Nine innings of unblemished scorebooks
Tops and bottoms
Naturally the single hit Hippo yielded
In the bottom of the tenth
Came around to score

Tall Texan southpaw
Ace of the Cubs
Magnificent seven summers
Good hurler
Bad luck
Ugly nickname

THE GRAY EAGLE

Tris perched in shallow center
Like a bird of prey
Taking off on wings for any fly
Soaring with his back to the infield
With uncanny rehearsed instinct
Ballhawk threw out runners
With deadly accuracy
And in record numbers
Texan in his own league
Speaker
COVERED
Centerfield

Sharp eye at the plate
Same speed that
Ran down would-be hits
Stretched plenty of singles
Into two-baggers
Tris might have been tagged
Baseball's Mister Double

If Adams had been stung
By the Boston outfield trio's arms
Instead of the Cubbie DP combo
Tris might have wound up
Immortalized in verse between
Hooper and Lewis

But Tris Speaker
Was not about might-have-beens
His deeds at bat and afield
Over twenty-two summers
Played fierce and proud
As an eagle

SHOELESS JOE

How he loved her
How he used her

She was never heavy to him
But the perfect fit
What a pair they were
Summer after summer:
Joe and Betsy

He called her black and beautiful
She responded to his touch
By springing to life
Charm for no one but Joe

Travelled with him from Philly
To Cleveland to Chicago
Betsy brought him luck
Until that terrible day
They were split up
By the Mountain Man

Cut down in his prime
Accusations hurled by gamblers
Jackson said it wasn't so
Betsy protested loudly
But the hanging judge had spoken
The fatal word

Torn from his trademark and trade
Banished to roam the countryside
Aching with all his soul
For a reunion that would never happen

How he loved her
How he used her
She was everything to him
Betsy was never just
Joe's bat

SMOKY JOE

The nickname was perfect
Steam comparable to the Big Train
His summer dueling partner

The dream season of 1912
Hints at his stuff
Thirty-eight times he took the hill
Thirty-five times he was there at the end
Ten times unscored upon
Thirty-five victories in hand
Probably talked more about his
Fifteen extra-base hits
And .290 average

When a thumb injury
Finally forced him off the mound
Wood took some time off
Then declared himself
A ballplayer

The smoke changed directions
Now it was his bat on fire
For five more summers

Like only a handful of others
Including the Babe
Smoky Joe Wood might have made the Hall
For his deeds on the rubber
Or in the batter's box
Had he been inducted he probably
Would have talked more about his son
Pitcher for the Red Sox

THE OLD PROFESSOR

Casey learned the game
From the ancient Orioles
McGraw and Robinson
Learned how to get
From here to October
And what to do
When the world is a Series
And lightning is needed
To bring home the ring

Casey played the game
Like a daffy Dodger
Ex- and in-citing fans
Ch- and dis-arming umps
Clown with some clout
Stengel had a major-league eye
And knew when to wink

Casey taught the game
To the new Yankees
Mickey and Whitey and Gil and Yogi
To his kids
Taught them not to settle for
Seasons that ended in September
Taught in his own language
Those who would listen and decipher
Learned to win

You could look up
Casey Stengel
Through all of the pages
Between the fading of the dead ball
And the arrival of the Amazin' Mets
Casey's purgatory
After the bliss of his Bronx dynasty
You could look him up:
Just watch for the jester
Wearing the crown and the grin

STUFFY

John McInnis
Had the right stuff
And plenty of it
So the nickname
Was a natural

First-sack for Mack
In the Hundred-Thou Infield
Stuffy developed a taste
For .300 seasons
And games surrounded
By the bunting of October

Stubby by first baseman standards
New Englander also developed
His own style of playing the bag
One-handed grace
Record-making errorless pace
As he covered his space

Steadying influence
On two more crews
Sailing to glory:
Last Series winner
Anchored in Boston's harbor
Then Pirates' mate in '25
John McInnis was the stuff
Managers' dreams
Were made of

SUB

Carl Mays was nicknamed
For his famous sidearm delivery
But the tag could be stretched
To stand for the way his career
Is overshadowed by
The pitch he'd have loved to
Have back

Pitchers' mistakes usually cost
Runs or games
And if the games are crucial
Sometimes mistakes cost seasons
Carl Mays is remembered
Like Branca and Downing
And a handful of other hurlers
For throwing one particular pitch:
Not because it was converted
Into a famous hit
But because Carl's mistake
Cost the batter his life

But this Kentuckian was much more
Than a single fastball gone awry:
Strong arm helped the Bosox
Then the Yanks to two flags each

Led a league in wins and saves --
Same summer!
Won twenty or more five times --
For three different teams!
One of the best-hitting pitchers ever
Carl was also tough post-season

Ran silent, ran deep
Most of his innings came *after* the tragedy
Which says plenty about
This sub's ability to rise
Out of the depths

HONEST

Sometimes ballplayers get their nicknames
By doing nothing at all,
And sometimes that is
The hardest thing of all to do.

Ask Eddie Murphy,
Whose skill at hitting and catching
The dead ball
Took him far from the sandlots
Of Mathewson country.

That skill, some college,
And a friendship with infielder Collins
Made Eddie a mainstay on Connie Mack's
Dynastic A's, 1912-1915,
Put him on stage in a couple World Series.
His long climb inspired the folks back home
To honor him with a crystal bat,
Reminding Eddie of his roots.

Traded to the White Sox the same summer
They acquired another outfielder,
A superstar with a Hall of Fame nickname,
Shoeless Joe.
Eddie Murphy was ready in the pinch,
And in 1919 his astounding .486 average
And an on-base percentage never matched
By Cobb or Ruth
Helped the Sox make it to October's Game.

Eddie Murphy's sox stayed
As unblemished and clean as a glass bat,
"Better forgotten than remembered for a wrong,"
Said the fellow who *earned* the nickname
Honest Eddie.

DEACON

Everett Scott
Was a tough out --
Tough to get him out
Of the lineup, that is:
Before the Iron Horse's streak
Was the Deacon's

And the durable Hoosier
Did it the hard way,
No short cuts for shortstops
Hang in there on the spikes-high
Runners hell-bent on breaking up DPs
Or trying to steal the keystone --
Wasn't much of a target
At five-eight and a hundred-forty
But Scott was good enough to anchor
Five Series-bound infields

This Scott was no Boomer
Great in his own quiet way
Everett Scott just made the plays
It took to win pennants
His glovework records
Destined to be surpassed
Sure as his
1307

BULLET JOE

Rookie found himself twenty
And in a pennant race
Winning fourteen
For the Tall Tactician:
Connie knew Joe Bush
Was no busher
Sweet sixteen soph victories
Found them together again
For another October reward

First year with the Red Sox
There he was again
Fifteen 2.11 caliber bull's-eyes
En route to the 1918 gonfalon
And more play in the long shadows

First two summers in the Bronx
Two more red white and blue falls:
Forty-five notches on his gun
Backed up by his old mound partner
Now busting fences and records
With Ruthian gusto

Leslie Ambrose Bush
Tossed seventeen seasons
Till his ammunition ran out
Nearly five hundred duels in the sun
Markers along the trail
Of Bullet Joe

SAD SAM

Sorrowful Sage from Woodsfield
Sam Jones made AL hitters sorry
Twenty-two summers straight
Almost pitched for the cycle:
Tour of duty with six of eight clubs

Fans' hurler:
Went five years without throwing
Waste pitches to first

Cleveland sent him to Boston
In exchange for a Gray Eagle
With plenty of flight time left:
But for one season, at least
Sad Sam made the trade seem fair --
Sweet sixteen wins helped the Bosox
Celebrate in 1918
Sitting on top of the world

Earned the downcast nickname
Wearing his cap low over his eyes
Like a gambler
Calculating odds:
What he held
Versus batters' cuts
Every pitch a new deal
Ball fours wild
Aces and jokers win
Crackling curves earned him another:
Horsewhips

Takes characters to earn monikers:
Sam Jones from the hills of Ohio
Collected them
Like tickets to the next team
And World Series rings

OL' STUBBLEBEARD

Burleigh was surly
His spitters no crimes
The last of the legals
Ol' Stubblebeard Grimes

He had the demeanor
Of Billy Goat Gruff
His pitches were weighted
With plenty of stuff

Intimidation
Was his middle name
Bullied his pass
To the game's Hall of Fame

Burleigh saw baseball
As kaleidoscope matter
Subtle in patterns
But no use for the batter

Durable thrower
He mixed in choice curves
Batting up against Grimes
Was a battle of nerves

We can only guess how
He'd have played his career
With one fewer pitch
To stick in your ear

THE SIZZLER

Toss a shutout against Walter Johnson
Hit four hundred twice
Get more hits in a season
Than anyone before or since
Play your position with elegance
Regularly leading your league
In assists and DPs
Steal fifty
Do all that and more
And they might compare you to
George Sisler

His Cooperstown bat required more games
Than pitching would permit
So he made the Ruthian switch
One less southpaw in the rotation
But oh that grace in the field
And prowess in the daily lineup

George was the guy who seemed quiet
By Roaring Twenties standards
His 41 was the league's streak mark till Joe D
Eclipsed like the .420 that he
Painted with strokes of genius
Forty-two ounce brush
On horsehide canvas
Humbly initialed
The other George H.

BAMBINO

Season by season
Swat by swat
Without TV
With only newsreel movies
And press headlines
The Babe escaped boxscore
Sports section
Sport -- and grew into folk hero

Conformity was a pitch he sent sailing
Ruth was as hard to manage by pitchers
(Or batters, when he was on the hill)
As by coaches and teammates
Everyday life became a mix
Of legend and events
Called shots and cured tots
Swirling among those Ruthian numbers

More popular than presidents
The Babe was permitted and forgiven all
For being wealthy when most were poor
Brash when most were meek
For being a rebel without a cause
Except the old ball game

Ruth confirmed with his crowns and titles
That America needed no royalty but his own
Anyone could make superstar
If that ugly saloon-keeper's kid
Who winked like a con man
Could wash the sport's black sox clean

Season by season
Swat by swat
He grew in our imagination and childlike eyes
By being himself
Standing against that profound current
Which would make us all less

RAJAH

He took his stand
As distant from the pitcher
As he could possibly be
Without being outside
The white rectangle
Waited
Focused
With eyes he reserved
(No moving picture shows --
Or reading)
Saved for that horsehide
Bound to be ambushed
On its trip to the mitt
Doomed to be converted into
Another counter in the
H column to the right of
Hornsby's name in
Tomorrow's box score

In the family album
Rogers' place is as secure
As his niche in Cooperstown
As certain as his name
In any hot stove debate
About the greatest hitter
Ever

But somehow we are quick to turn the page
Move on to faces less stern
Uncles far less successful
Or who drank too much
They left behind kind memories

Hornsby stares at us
From his swirling world of
Unthinkable sums of money
Betting on the horses
Getting on the nerves
Of everyone in his path

As if he is still taking a stand
As distant from us
As he can possibly be
Without being outside
This imperfect clan

MEMPHIS BILL

Who knows what he'd have done
If baseball was his life
And not just his livelihood?

This cream of a hitter
Rose to the top of the game
Slowly: rookie at 27
Firstbasemen in New York
Had to be superstar material
And Bill Terry fit the bill fine

We remember him for his glove
As well as that scorching bat
That made his home park opponents
Wish they had Polo horses
To chase his liners in the gaps

In that wild summer of the Bat
When practically everyone hit .300
Terry hit .4(01) --
Last in his league to ascend
That privileged peak

Who knows what he'd have done
Had he been on speaking terms
With his boss
Those two silent seasons?
Yet McGraw named Terry
To carry on the Giant fight
And add to their NL flag collection

We remember Manager Bill for asking
If Brooklyn was still in the league
(New York turns whispers into headlines)
And for playing in the majors as if
He was ready to be called up

PIE

Rhymes with eye
As in batting
Look up contact hitter
And Traynor will be there
Sure as he was there
Turning the smash over the bag
From a double to a five-three
With a hunk of leather
That deserved no assist on the play

In a city with its own way of talking
Pie never lost his
Over seventeen loyal seasons
Pittsburgh adopted him
Like a favorite son

He was no specialist
So his batsmanship
Baserunning and feats afield
Guarding the hot corner
All glow equally
From our distance

The Game's greatest third baseman?
Calling Pie the best would not
Swell his head then
Nor add to his stature now
He carved out his Cooperstown niche
Like a Robert Frost spinning a poem
With quiet dignity
Hard work
Grace
Leaving behind a sport
That now spoke
With a little of his accent

GABBY

Grew up on a farm team
Oldest of fourteen kids
Took after his dad
Then went beyond --
Charles Leo Hartnett
Wasn't really gabby
But sure knew how to give fans
Something to gab about

For nearly twenty summers
Gabby quarterbacked Cub pitchers
Earning with his mates
Four fingers' worth of Series rings

Cannon arm to blow enemy runners
Back to their dugouts
Armored knight defended
Home castle with noble might
In his own battles aplate
Swung his mace with .300 grace
And dragon-slaying power

In a career of hard labor
Mountain carved day by day
Pitch by pitch
Into a proud Rushmore
Of Cooperstown dimensions --
Backstop of ironic nickname lingers brightest
In our overburdened memory
For a single swing:
Rookie manager stood in --
Sun going down on pennant hope
And the Cubs' twenty-game win streak
Pirates one strike away
When Gabby snatched victory
With a shot in the dark
Sending the Bucs into the gloamin'
And setting Chicago afire for October's game

HACK

Shape all his own
Wilson looked like he'd been squeezed
Bottom up from his size six shoes
So that his chest and arms bulged
Surged with dynamite
Did he even have a neck?

Lewis Robert Wilson entered the world
In the year of the new century
Entered the game as a Giant of NY
But didn't roar in the twenties
Until he joined the Cubs

Over five straight summers
Mr. Wilson hacked increasing numbers
Of increasingly long home runs
Peaking in that infamous hitter's summer

Sawed-off shotgun swinger
Chicago hit man
Blasted two double-barrel marks
That still survive:
Fifty-six round-trippers
Hundred and ninety-one RBIs

To a National League ear
Numbers that sound like Ruth's sixty
Or DiMaggio's fifty-six:
Sublime, magnificent, wondrous
Divine digits
Worth a shrine of their own
Made folks forget
Five foot six

Hack Wilson was human
And battled more than pitchers
Heavy hitter and drinker
Outside the lines he was losing
And sliding

And suddenly Hack was going
Headed out like one of his clouts
Going like beer spilled
Into the ivy at Wrigley

Gone at forty-eight:
Number so much smaller
Than fifty-six
When we remember Hack Wilson

LEFTY

Four decades before Carlton
Five years before Gomez
Appeared the southpaw
Known ever since as Lefty

Work in the coal mines
Fueled his catapult blazers;
Blowing glass taught him
The fine artistry of curves
And the symmetry
Reflected some in his
Precisely three hundred wins
And an equal number of games finished

Grove in the groove:
Backbone of the rotation and
Awesome as the A's dynastic offense
In those three splendid seasons
Philly escaped depression --
When they ruled the AL
Murdering the Bronx row --
Lefty's 31 in '31
(Following 28 in the Year of the Hitter)
The perfect harmonious climax
For patriarch Cornelius' crew

Cochrane's one finger down
Meant ornery fast balls
White grapes of wrath
From the terrible swift hurler
With the matching disposition
Lefty and losing didn't mix:
Stand back when they
Shared the same locker

Fellers like Koufax, Nolan and Roger the Rocket
Stir in our memories the smooth warm light of
Robert Moses Grove's fiery left arm

BUCKETFOOT AL

Simmons roared in with the Twenties
Solid as Shibe's concrete and steel
He became a royal member
Of Mack's second dynasty
Forming with Foxx and Cochrane
A terrorist trio of Killer A's

Al's bucketfoot stance
Drew skeptical chuckles
Only until the game was afoot
As his long bat lashed out
Sprays of long liners
The flaw became a warning:
This pale Pole showed no mercy
In the war he declared
On all hurlers

Snapshots of this warrior
Are all slightly blurred:
His snare of the long fly
That tried to be Gehrig's
Fifth homer that game --
Crucial late-inning clouts
(Sleeves flapping on the slides)
Or October thunder --
Even his notable K
In Hubbell's starry string
Remind us of how this man
Hit

MEAL TICKET

With King Carl
We have choices

Remember him for his mass murder
(Ruth Gehrig and Foxx on twelve tosses)
Of the row of stars in '34?
Or for throwing the game's longest whitewash
Same year he put 46 straight goose-eggs up
On the enemy's scoreboard?
Or for the no-hitter or the
Twenty glorious innings in the '33 Series or the
Pair of MVPs?

With King Carl
We have choices

Unlike those who faced him in combat
They had to try hitting
The screwball from the south side
Dipping and snapping on the black edges
Control sharp as that broken glass
From the water cooler shattered
By the freak pitch's latest victim

With King Carl
We have choices

Unlike those who considered him
For enshrinement in Cooperstown --
McGraw's left arm
Hell, the game's best in the 30's
Perhaps the higher tribute was paid
By his Giants' opponents
Who crowded their dugout steps
When Hubbell pitched
To watch
And marvel
Like fans

MECHANICAL MAN

His lack of color
Was legendary
All he did was
Hit throw and field
With the All-Star efficiency
Of a machine

Charlie Gehringer was a
Vacuum at the keystone
Turn him on and he
Keeps his turf clean
With monotonous consistency
Preventing build-up on the basepaths
Sweeping away enemy rallies
Making it look effortless

Charlie Gehringer was a
Robobatter at the plate
Turn him on and he
Sorts out the pitches
Worth his swings
Automatically
Racks up two hundred safeties a season
Drives in a hundred or so
And all with such showmanship
That come time to vote for MVP
You scratch your head for his name
This Tiger roared
With his leather and wood

COOL PAPA

Legend has him racing his own hits
To second base
Faster than the speed of light
Going out in the bedroom
Scoring from first
On bunts
Stealing two bases
On a pitchout
A sprinter whose feats
Inspired mythic tales
And grew in the telling

Anchor man Jackie
And Monte
And all to whom Bell passed
The black baton
Finished the relay

Fitting that the man who was
A blur on the basepaths
Should become a symbol for
A page in the sport's history
Blurred itself
By tears and wonderings
Of what might have been

Look up speed in the baseball dictionary:
Cool Papa Bell has already been there
And is sliding past your finger
Around your tag
Can't touch him
To score

His seasons were filled with movement
Dusty bus trips between towns
Made longer by the searches
For places where blacks were welcome
To eat or sleep or be
Made longer by the searches

For clean socks and sweatshirts
To wear in the third game of the day
Made longer by the searches
For the day when all their deeds afield
Might be written down
In scorebooks and newspapers
Might be written
In black and white
Might be dignified
By the recognition
They happened

IRON HORSE

What's in a nickname?
Lou's was
A tale of two eras

The horse was power
Before planes trains and automobiles
Natural brawny native
Tame to the eye but always wild
Galloping past broken-down buggies
To spaces where no tracks had been laid

Iron had its virtues
Durable hard strong
Locomotive stuff
Crossing the land without rest
Putting towns and cities on the map

The Iron Horse took the field
Season after shining season
Enduring as no one before or since

His accomplishments in the game
Hardly suggest a career
Cut short
His final seasons spent courageously
Slugging against an invisible hurler
A disease destined to strike out
"The luckiest man on the face of the earth"

Iron rusts and horses die
We know all that
Yet Gehrig's words jar and haunt us
Our nickname
Was supposed to
Let him play
Forever

BLACK MIKE

Once upon a time
Catchers
Were armored backstops
Not expected to hit and run
And push their teams to win
With the fury of a general
In love with trench warfare

Mickey Cochrane
Raged to pennants
With MVP fire in his eyes
The A's of Connie Mack
And then his own Tigers

The teams caught *him*

What ended that day in May
When Mickey's skull was suddenly split
By the high inside heater?
The summers of .300 swings
In combat focused squarely on victory
His squatting battle cries silenced
Energy spent at last
His mark on the game
Etched indelibly

BIG POISON

Romulus & Remus were twins born to myth
Wilbur & Orville flew to fame together
But in baseball, brothers must prove themselves
Detached

Little Lloyd and Paul
Grew up pitching and knocking
Oklahoma corncobs with hoe handles
So baseballs with bats seemed easy pickings

Paul headlined this brother act
Scattering his punchlines
All across Forbes' outer stage:
Gaps protected inning tops
Were his in the bottoms
Their local run of fourteen seasons
Kept their city in the spotlight
Even if for just one October encore

One story has it
The Pirate pair got the tags
From a *person* with a Flatbush accent
Before uniforms bore names

The elder Waner led their
Record-making hit parade
Swinging with Glee
(His middle name)
Into the golden club of
Three-thousanders

Literally double trouble
Opponents were regularly stung
By the fleet leadoff scorpion's singles
Then snakebit by the right fielder
Uncoiling and rattling the wall
While their hurler groped for
The antidote

PEPPER

Memorize his face during BP
Once the game is on
His uniform will be no help
In identifying this smiling fellow:
The top will be the shade of the infield dirt
Even in front
From thieving belly-flops
The legs dusty and green
Stained from sliding shoe-lace grabs
Of would-be Texas-leaguers

Memorize his name, too
Because you won't find it
In the scorecard
Or tomorrow's box score:
John Leonard Roosevelt
Salt of the Gashouse Gang
Martin was pure Pepper

Charlie Hustle of his day
Pepper spiced up the show
For his Cardinal teammates
Between and outside the lines
"Wild Hoss of the Osage"
Left Frisch holding the reins

The stats he bequeathed
Seem too ordinary to be his
All too bland -- save one:
Has anyone else
Who has visited the Series
Risen to that challenge
Quite so smartly?
His dozen hits sunk the A's in '31 --
One less safety in '34
Pepper: .418 for two Octobers
Seasoning of the winning recipes

THE LIP

Leo was not a nice guy
No matter where he finished
In his half century with the Game

His glove was mightier than his bat
Captain of the Gashouse
Never just one of the Gang
That might have been his epitaph
But he lived on

Skipper in Flatbush
He was Ensign Pulver cast as Queeg
And finally as Ahab
Destined to help Jackie aboard
And shatter the Great White
That might have been his epitaph
But he lived on

When he made the short jump of ships
He found himself at the helm
For Thomson's round-the-world cruise
And for the arrival of a real Giant:
Willie was destined to bring fame
To whomever penciled in his name
That might have been Durocher's epitaph
But he lived on

On into his fifties and sixties
Into the sixties and seventies
Leo penciled in nearly four thousand lineups
Might have been around at the end of more games
But for his amplifying Lip
And because he lived on and on
We have our choice of words
For this man of choice words
For Leo Durocher's epitaph

BROTHER RICK

Durable Durham bull
Kept catching and catching
And catching --
Rick Ferrell was a
First division backstop
On second division teams
Until he joined Cooperstown's

How many games of catch
With young Wes
And five other brothers
Do you suppose Rick played?

All prelude
To eighteen seasons at the top

Might have made the Hall
For longevity in the squat position
Double-duty solid hitting
Eye for sifting balls from strikes

Or for performance beyond the call:
Handling a starting rotation
Of four knuckleballing Senators!
Rick *still* made catching
Look easy

SATCHEL

The very names of his teams
Stir up other-worldly visions:
Birmingham Black Barons
Nashville Elite Giants
Chattanooga Black Lookouts
Crawfords and Monarchs
Stars and the Black Sox
Who weren't turned out
But never let in either

The very names of his pitches
Stir up colorful visions:
Little Tom and Long
Radio and B Balls
Two-hump blooper
And the hesi-
Tation

In a game where records
Are part of the mystique
Satchel's birth date was uncertain
Seemed like he was born pitching
And destined to throw forever
Always with style
His own

Even then, in his four decades
Mostly in the shadows
Before the awful eclipse ended
There was no one like
Lanky Leroy Paige
Don't bother to look back

Did that oldest rookie ever die
Or does he live on yet
Folk hero separate but equal
Always somewhat separate
Always at least equal

BILL

When Bill Dickey's fingers talked
Pitchers listened
And the Yankees won

Ruth and DiMaggio got the headlines
Bill Dickey got broken fingers
And the Yankees won

Man of quiet consistency
He was there behind the plate
While the dynasty changed casts

Talked more with his bat and glove
He swung and slung with slashing power
Hit in the clutch
And the Yankees won

Roomed with Gehrig
And was first to learn
Of that other iron man's secret:
We can only guess
How this gentle giant
Replied

Fitting that Bill Dickey
Played himself in
Pride of the Yankees:
Because that title
Stood for much more than Lou

When Bill Dickey caught for the Yankees
Baseball won

DOUBLE X

Jimmie slugged X-rated homers
Renowned more for their violent sound
Than their prodigal trajectory

Protege of H.R. Baker
Schooled in Connie Mack's dugout
Until he burst forth
With a dozen summers
Of thirty-plus power
Beastly biceps on display
And delivering

Intimidating from the on-deck circle
Foxx amplified the force
Of those fortunate to bat ahead
Simmons at Shibe
Or Ted in the Monster's shadow
Enemy pitchers saw the approach
Of Jimmie's broad shoulders
Imagined his long strides
And pondered the containment
Of the impending blast

The extra X marked the spot
In Chicago and Cleveland and New York
And almost every AL park
Where the tape-measure stopped
And the tales started

Include this gentle giant
With Gehrig and Greenberg and Mize
In any hot stove debate about
Who's on First
Forever

BUCK

If Josh was the black Babe
Buck Leonard was the Iron Horse
Of the Negro Leagues

First-class mittwork
Compared to Chase & Sisler
Batwork incomparable
Anchorman of the Grays
Led Homestead to the home stretch
As dependably as the Yankees' Lou

While the Clipper sailed in the Bronx
And the Splinter perked up the Fen
Buck slugged for his team
In one pennant race after another
Nine straight flags!
Lighting up his league
Opening Days to the Series' finales
Thundering with Twin Gibson
Blooming and booming
For his Magna Cum Posey manager

No doubt how Buck would have done
Had he been the color of the ball
Because when he got his chances
In exhibitions
The Buck stopped fear
And put on a show

The stories that survive suggest
Josh and Buck
Played in a league of their own
No matter where or whom against

Sixty cents a day for meals
Rooming houses instead of hotels
Slept two abed in Pullmans
On the road trips
Sometimes paid five dollars a game

Their path to Cooperstown
Was long and winding
Hot and dusty
Over the back roads of the sport

Which the greater tragedy?
That their glorious play was denied
National spotlight and recognition?
Or that baseball itself is poorer forever
Without more memories of these men
When they were at the top of their game?

RED

Voice was comfortable
And as welcome in your parlor
As a relative come to visit

Part of the family
Southern accent rubbed off
Red Barber made listening fans
Feel they had the best seats
At the ball park

Story-teller
Poet
Play-by-play man
Who never forgot
To tell the score

Dignified his profession
Set standards
Spiced up games with
Lyrical expressions
Taught the game new words

'Old Redhead talked to us
Might be on the road
But he sounded right at home
Made us care about the game
He was reporting
And about the Game

Turned our radios into TVs
Let us see each pitch
Follow the ball after the batcracks
Turned our living rooms
Bedrooms and cars
Into extensions of the grandstand
Our silent or loud cheers and groans
Blended with those in the background
As Red talked to us

BILLY

Named for the orator
This William Jennings Bryan
Spoke with a golden glove
And stick --
Billy Herman
Was keystone class
In the thirties

His decade at Wrigley
Marked by a Cub trio
Of trips to October's Game:
Billy pushed his teams home
Like the leadoff batters
He hit-and-ran behind
With singular skill

Wood talked trouble
For enemy moundsmen:
Often double trouble

Leather lectured long
With undebatable fielding feats
Dialectic DPs
Put-outs polemic
And assertive assists

But no controversy
About Billy Herman's
Silver niche
In the game's story --
Peerless leader
As player
And story-teller

BUCKY

For William Henry Walters
Life in baseball was lovelier
Second time around

Boston infielder
Both leagues
Didn't throw a pitch
Till his fourth summer in the bigs
Cincinnati Red turned out to be his color
Red flags in '39 and '40
When Bucky was the red-hot ace
Throwing sidearm fire

In his first post-season games
Bucky was stung by the Yanks
Twice:
No hitting behind him in Game Two
No fielding in Game Four
As the Reds were swept away

But the second time around
In the ring with Detroit
Walters scored the one-two punches:
First a three-hitter at home
Then a back-to-the-wall must-win
Sixth Game shutout
(With a homer to boot)
As the Reds came back
To win in Seven

Walters pitched through the war years
Toured Europe off-season with the USO
Morale-booster even out of uniform
Philadelphian threw a mean sinker
But Bucky himself
Was unsinkable

MASTER MELVIN

It must have been love at first sight:
The dead-pull hitting kid
Just over his first glimpse of New York
Standing at the plate and gazing
With wonder and delight
To where the Polo Grounds' right field ended
Less than a hundred yards away
There lay what for two decades
Would be known as Ottville

Time was on his side
No need to rush things
The teen had time to go to school
On the bench beside Mr. McGraw
Time to ease into the lineup
To start making history

The energy he saved up
Signing autographs --
Six letters and Next, please --
Poured into his game:

Eccentric but disciplined
High-kicking right leg
Pounding down as the pitch is studied
Arcing bat springing around
For the launch;
Marvelous snares and snags
When he roamed far from McGraw's dugout
Yet within armshot of the base ahead
Of the larcenous runners
Arrested by his gun

Mel Ott was a sixty-nine inch tall
Hundred and seventy pound Giant
Pitchers would just as soon walk him
Rather than face his game-breaking
Unmistakable presence

SMILING STAN

"If you can't stand the heat
Stay off the hot corner" --
So the saying might have gone
If Stan Hack had coined it

Sixteen summers in the heat
Of four pennant-capped races,
Of Wrigley's magnifying glass,
Of .301-degree swinging,
Made Cub fans smile

Stan made friends
As easily as he slashed hits
That brought teammates around --
One of the best ever
At getting on base,
He was no Hack (Wilson),
But Stan had no lack
Of winning stuff

Game 6 of the 1935 Series
Score tied
Stan led off with a triple
And was stranded --
Minutes before
The home team pushed across
The winning run

Stranded again
In Hall of Fame balloting,
Stan Hack's photo
In baseball's family album
Nevertheless
Smiles
For all time

DIZZY

Shooting star
He flashed so loudly and brightly
In his abbreviated time before us
That the impression was lasting

He may indeed have been the greatest
As he said
For that time
Cockiness enough to fill a Gashouse
His fireballs backing up his brags
And making his predictions come true

The X-rays lied:
Plenty in Dean's bean, all right
Some of it slud out later over the radio
A lot of it got packaged
But the bulk was focused
On Cardinal foes digging in
Turning ABs into Ks

His last game is a clue to the character:
Challenged out of retirement
Out from behind his famous mike
A decade after his All-Star toe
Dampened his glowing arm
He started tossing goose eggs all over again
Just for show
Just for *the* show
Till his hamstringed body
Made him quit all over again

Never a case of mind over matter
For Diz
But a matter of minding
How the matter was encased
If he said something was gold
It was damn well going to glitter

HAMMERIN' HANK

Before Jackie broke the color line
Hank hammered at similar stuff
Learning when to take
And when to swing
On and off the diamond

Greenberg's might
Produced a storm of Tiger runs
Near-record summers of
Round-trippers and ribbies

His career almost suggests
That the answer to
"How do you get to Cooperstown?"
Is: "Practice, practice, practice!"

When the Tigers needed first base
For Rudy York
Hank could relate to that --
Needing first base
Was why he chose Detroit
Over the Stadium
Where Gehrig ruled

This team player
Could not ride the bench
In the battles after Pearl Harbor
His Air Corps heroics
Grandly recalled after the struggle
When his slam in the final '45 game
Took his team into the Series

Greenberg was a giant
An awkward kid from the Bronx
Who grew into a polished pro
A Goliath with the soul of David

JOSH

There's more about him that we don't know
Than what we know

We know he played the game hard
His black power
Generating as many stories and legends
As long balls
Hits that dared to go
Where no horsehide had gone before

His Grays and Crawfords were teams
To reckon with
'Specially when Satchel was throwing
Radio balls and B-balls
And Buck Leonard batted cleanup

If only the doors had opened sooner
Maybe we would recall Babe
As the white Josh Gibson

ARKY

Wagner's protege
And heir to his slice of the turf
Vaughan could do it all
But quietly

Arky's bat
Rippled with triples
And painted .300 seasons
With constancy and verve
His Mona Lisa 1935
Still shimmers and dazzles

Arkansas polished gem
That displayed its facets best
On the All-Star diamonds
Hard substance
On collision course
With the Lip of Brooklyn

Had the patience for ball fours
And the eye to spoil fouls
Would rather retire at 31
Support the war on his farm
Than give in to Durocher
Stayed off stage for over three
Prime seasons
For his own unstated
Prime reasons

In uniform
We only saw a man at work
Out of it
We saw a man who wanted to decide
Himself
Who he'd call Boss
That's important to some folks

THE BIG CAT

Clawed his mark
Into every park
Eyes sharp as the crack
Of the booming bat
Reflexes to terrorize
And play with his hurler prey

Who's on first
When Johnny Mize is in town?
Lefty slugger with a flair
For the multi-homer game
Crushes them too
Yet can lay off those tempters
So you might toss him more gophers
Than third strikes

Who's on first?
First nine summers
He dealt the Cards
And then the Giants
Diamond days of .300
(Club smote fifty-one in forty-seven)
Fans' hearts wild
For the perennial
Triple Crown threat

Dogs may be man's best friend
But give any manager
The Big Cat

Give him to Casey
As his lives on the nine wound down
Let him lurk in the shadows of the bench
Stalk the pitcher with predator eyes
Until the pinch
Then spring
Stun
Like a king of the beasts

Lionize Mize
For holding his own
A decade and a half
In the Golden Age of First Basemen
And for shining some
In the October shadows of Yankee Stadium
When he had to be good
This Johnny was

AS IN WRECK

Couldn't tell the players
Without a scorecard
Till Veeck wrote on the jerseys

Once he came along
Couldn't trust the scoreboard
Anymore either --
Might just explode on you
Like fireworks after last outs
Or a disco demolition disaster

And beware birthday cakes bearing midgets --
Eddie Gaedel looks cute but
Might just get in the game

Who knows who he'll sign next?
Larry Doby or ageless Satchel
Bill Veeck hustled in the front office
Like a Cobb on basepaths
Tradition and status quo look out
For the maverick owner
With a fan's love for the game
And the instincts of Barnum

Veeck lost a leg in the South Pacific
But returned to create Bali Ha'i
In Cleveland and St Louis and Chicago
Providing many an enchanted evening
Lots of happy talk
And a few World Series as well

Who knows what will happen when the boss
Mingles in the bleachers and grandstands?
Might discover more ways to fill a stadium
Than anyone had imagined before
Winning teams would do it
But so would making games so much fun
That fans couldn't afford to stay home

The establishment hated him for trying
Everything under the sun and the lights
(Even morning games for wartime swing shifts)
But in the end they had to admit
Veeck was carefully teaching them
The future

YANKEE CLIPPER

Joe D. was born in 1914
Same as my Dad
Who's long gone now

Joe's still with us
Although that song keeps asking
Where he's gone
As if he has
As if we'd ever let him
Be lost to memory

Joe D. played center stage
Center city
When baseball was center sport
There his style and class
Refracted the limelight
Like a perfectly cut diamond

The Streak
Was like that final burst
Of color and illumination
At the finish
Of a 4th of July fireworks show
Perfect for timeless association
With Mr. Consistency

Joe D. was born on November 25
Like my Little Leaguer son
Any father would be proud
To see DiMaggio's thing reflected
Even a little
In his offspring
Not the numbers
But the consistent effort
Poise in the noise
Uncommon grace
Presence
Old-fashioned pride in his work

DUTCH MASTER

Five June days
In his twenty-third summer
Guaranteed his name
A permanent niche
In the sport's memory
Johnny Double No-Hit
Vander Meer

No-no's are stewed
In pressure cookers
The late-inning tension
Growing more terrible by the pitch
Isolating the hurler
Silencing his dugout
Causing the noise in the stands
To pulsate in exaggerated whoops
For each fresh out
Then each strike
Finally to burst
With relief
The collective pain
Of birthing
Over

Just once so far
Has the game bore twins

Under Ebbets' vogue lights
Johnny on the spot
This time from the get go
Prepared from his first high hard one
To tip his hat and celebrate again
His notable nine
When the end inevitably arrived

Instead
Here we go again
Flirting time

Double the tension
Triple the collective pain
But multiply by forty thousand
Cheering in the waiting room
The joy of delivery
Cigars all around
For the Dutch Master

COUNTRY

Enos made that Chicago word
Slaughter
Congenial to St Louis
Easy to spot on the field
The man in motion
Hustling extra bases
Spraying clutch hits
Corner to corner

In the clan's album
Enos is the relative
We are tempted to remember
By a single photograph
One war over
Another to wage
His furious race home
Series-winning run strapped
On his bent back
Warrior back where he belonged
Tasting victory
In the charge

Gingerly we tuck behind that picture
Smaller ones
His Southern discomfort
With the family's first
Interracial marriage:
Failed strike
Successful spike --
Not to hide them
But to secure them better
Lest we forget

Not just some
But all of the pictures
Of Enos' life
Suggest the nickname
Country

GUNNER

Bob Prince's voice
Was reflected in his sport coats:
Colorful and loud
Mostly original
Above all comfortable

The sandpaper sound carried farther
(The wind was a factor)
Than Dick Stuart's homers
To Pirate fans in exile from the 'Burgh
Or the friendly confines of Forbes
Connecting them
With the battlefront

His nicknames stuck like superglue
Making the players a little more familiar
And the game a little more fun

Sometimes he was so full of --
Baseball Stuff --
That you became so mad
You wanted to heave your scorebook
Through the radio
But you couldn't
And then he made you feel
Like you were in the upper deck
On the other end of a Stargell slam
And when he finally trotted out
"We had 'em ALLLLL the way"
You were laughing and crying
And wondering what time to tune in
Tomorrow night

Every house that KDKA reached became
A House of Thrills
Not by a gnat's eyelash either
Or the length of a green weenie
But by a country mile

We can never quite kiss goodbye
The echoes of his calls
Any more than we can forget
The way we were
When we just listened
To partner-in-banter Possum
And that son of a Gunner
Who made every game
A home game

THE MAYOR OF WRIGLEY FIELD

Took his time
To lumber around the bases
Or the outfield --
Moved slowly into his role
As ML slugger --
30-30 "rookie" in '48:
35 dingers, at age 31!

Hank Sauer's sweet swing
Came into its own
When weighted properly
With a 40-ounce Hafey model --
Jewel of an idea
Led to a 50-point crown
And a ticket to the show

Exchange of uniforms
(Cincy for Chicago --
Picked up for Peanuts and a Hat!)
Led to the next level of Fame:
Exchanging his long pokes
With the bleacher folks
For tobacco packets
And between-inning banter
Over the backyard ivy fence

Dutch master of clout
From the Iron City
Racked up nearly 200 notches
On that over-sized bat
First seven Cubbie summers

All-Star and MVP of the League
Hank was that and more at Wrigley
Nearly two mayoral terms --
Had to have power
To rule Cook County
Had to shake a lot of hands
To capture hearts

To send fans for a loop
To send them home feeling like
They'd seen a World's Fair
Instead of just Hank Sauer's
Big shoulders

RAPID ROBERT

On his Iowa farm
His father planted a home plate
And a pitching rubber
Seeds that produced
A Cooperstown arm

Young Bob threw every day
Winters in the barn
Helped build a real Field for Dreams
Grandstand behind first
Scoreboard for the zeroes
And finally he came

Cy was no Shoeless Joe
Scout offered only a buck
And a baseball full of names
With room for one more
Bob's ticket East

Cleveland's Rapid Transit
To runs at October
Official scorers' panacea
Just stamp the book with K's

His missing seasons
Were spent throwing in loyal Navy blue
Not just entertaining his uncle's kids
But hurling against enemy strikers in the Pacific
In an opposite reality

When Feller's heat was turned up
Safeties became endangered
In three games extinct
In a dozen others reduced to one

Was it velocity
That made this Indian a winner:
Veering white
Mixed up with dead man curves?
Or was it something else from the farm
Grown up inside the boy
Good stuff
Of manhood

THE KID

Final day of the season
The choice is to sit it out
And go down in history with the handful
Of .400 hitters
Or play the doubleheader

The numbers that spell Ted best
May be that six-for-eight
Knocked out while on the ledge
Baseball immortality on the line
Crux of a legend
Williams accepted the dare

Too much for a single nickname
Splinter for opposing arms
Splendid for the Fenway swarms
Seemed a veteran of foreign war
Even before Korea
Triple-Crown Thumper
Who had to have the
Last turn at bat
In Teddy's Ballgame

JACKIE

When his name comes up
We always see Robinson in our mind's eye
Dancing off third

His own eyes fixed on the windup
He's ready to go
Electricity
Poised to shock and thrill
Dust never settling near his cleats
He's wired to break
Steal a run or a game
To win

Of course
It's the riskiest move in the game
But he was used to dares
Hero or goat
Once he said Yes to Mr. Rickey
He was destined to be one or the other
Stealing home must have seemed
Child's play
To Jackie
A chance to move on
Instead of just endure

First black man in the Promised Land
Modern Moses delivering in the clutch
His rookie season screamed
To the pharaohs of the game:
Let my people play

Barrelling down the line
Parting seas of bigotry
His dash home
Could no longer be blocked
His dark finger on the white
Spelling victory
For everyone

PISTOL PETE

Proved he was big-league
Was Brooklyn Dodger material
When he crashed the Elmira wall
Strike one
But call up Pete Reiser

Batting champ at twenty-two
Self-taught switch-hitter
Played center because
That's where there was room
Pete was dazzling on the
Wall-less basepaths
Especially thefty
Of the five-sided plate

Pennant Race '42
Dodgers dueling in St. Louis
Extra innings
None on but the game
Just about out of useable daylight
When Slaughter connected
Reiser sprinted to Sportsman's deep
Somehow reached the descended sphere
Strike two
Ball and game jarred loose
As Country hustles home
Beginning of the end for the Brooklyns

After the war, Pistol Pete came back
But not really --
Still hopeful in '47 until
Strike three

Each time outfielders tread warning tracks
And bang into padded perimeters
They ought to thank that strikeout victim
Who would run through brick walls
For a catch

THE MAN

As kids we copied everything big league
Willie's basket catches
Spahnie's high-kicking delivery
Maz' twin-killing pivot at the keystone
Then there was Stan's stance

We could imitate it all right
Peek out around the corner
Coiled question mark
Ready to explode into a double
Slash the up outside pitch over third
Or off the right-center scoreboard
Yank the low inside one
Over the screen in right

Never happened
What worked so well for Musial
The durable Cardinal
Was folly for us to try
We were posing
Trying to look like the hitter
The natural Man

Good thing he never played Little League
Coaches would have straightened him out
And the rest
As they say
Would not be history

HOLY COW!

Harry was Budweiserville's voice
For two and a half decades
Then Mayor of Rush Street
When colorizing Chisox and Cubs
Radio games:
Plain speaker, never detached
Last of the red-hot rooters

Caray was the Harry
Who gave us not hell
But heaven:
Midwest magnet attracting us close
To our portables or plug-ins
Tones reflecting the moments
Inning after game after season

Harry dared to hope out loud
Shared his disappointments
Love and hate
Crests of home-team-win ecstasy
Or depths of gloom in defeats

Broadcaster-showman
Pied-piper for fans
Looking for a good time
Harry stretched mid-7th celebration
Over each inning

Sarcastic banter with boothmates
Fish net ever ready for fouls
Told it like a fan:
Might be -- charged with potential
Could be -- full of possibility
Is -- the genuine article
No credibility gap
Between Harry Caray
And those fortunate to be
On the other end of the waves he made

PRINCE HAL

Local boy took a while
But when he made good
Hal Newhouser was royal

Sixth summer up
Tiger southpaw finally pounced
On back-to-back MVPs
Four score of wins in three seasons
Blazing brilliantly
During and after the war
In control at last

After two hundred W's for Detroit
Hal wound up his career
With the other Great Lakes franchise
Relieving Indian starters
Tribe on the warpath to the Series

Prince Hal's reign
Spangled with gems:
Fifth and seventh game
Cub trophies
October of '45 --
Armageddon '48 victory
Duel with Feller

Moral of his story may be
Good things come to him who
Waits:
Like the kiss
Thirty-some years after
The hanging of the spikes
That turned this Prince
Into a Hall of Famer

CAMPY

Don't call Roy
A Boy
Of Summer --
He was a man
Before he came to Brooklyn

Campanella's blackness
Meant he'd follow Josh
Instead of Cochrane or Dickey
But given the chance
Followed Jackie
Across the line

Marvel at the best .333 ever:
MVP three of nine summers!
Or at his consistent clout
Or his artful Dodger backstopping

Star before the majors
Saw his brilliance,
Star after tragedy struck --
Roy Campanella
Can never be spelled in numbers
Any more than soul
Can be painted
By body:
Campy caught
And was catching
Like the very game
That this man played in
And stayed in
So long and so well

SPAHNIE

The older this dog became
The more tricks he added

Overhand destroyer of timing
Spahn made winning twenty
A habit and a trademark

Veteran before rookie
As hard to root against
As he was to defeat

My own book on Spahnie
As a Pirate fan
Said to get to him early
Or wait till tomorrow

I looked forward in those days
To the All-Star games and the Series
When I could root for the NL ace
With a clear conscience

While he was climbing that hill toward 300
We kept thinking back to those empty years
Wondering if his over-seasons
Spent in the uniform of his Uncle
Would keep him from reaching the top

When he hit the peak
Without breaking stride
And kept climbing
We realized bravery in action
Was this guy's **thing**

After the Purple Heart
The Cy Young took on a perspective
His Cooperstown plaque
A more facile bronze than his
Star

THE WHIP

Six-six beanpole
Remembered most for
The way he threw
Ewell Blackwell
His name was within two outs
Of being linked forever
With Vander Meer

Wicked, nasty, vicious --
These were some of the printables
Right-handed batters used
To describe his sidearm slings

Swooshing in a white blur
From third base
Freezing
Intimidating
Backing off
When the whip cracked
Hitters listened

We saw only glimpses
Of what might have been
Had the whip not given out early:
Streak of sixteen wins
Topping the league in
Shutouts as a rookie
Strikeouts and wins
That second summer
When he just missed
The no-no-no-no

No matter -- from then on,
Whenever Blackwell
Took the hill for Cincinnati
The air hummed with possibilities
The way it's supposed to
In baseball

RALPH

Hero without a nickname
When New York had its Clipper
Boston its Splendid Kid
And St Louis its Man
Star without a galaxy
Pittsburgh's Ralph

Heir to Greenberg's Gardens and his wisdom
Kiner lit up and filled up Forbes
His first seven summers in the show
Topping the league in homers each season
Twice over the nifty fifty mark
Without a supporting cast
Ralph stole the show

Suddenly he was gone
"Traded" -- as if anyone
Could equal his worth
For those who clicked the turnstiles
Just for Ralph
Left behind were the echoes
Of Ruthian cracks
(With Ruthian frequency)
Aunt Minnie's broken windows
Adoring unending
Cheers

The sounds were long gone
Like a trademark hit
No joy in Iron City:
Pirate treasure overboard

YOGI

If this guy hadn't come along
The sport would have invented him

The mobile gnome
With a gift for one-liners
That brought down the house
And roundhouse liners
That filled up the seats
Most Octobers

Yogi was the positive end
Of the New York batteries
That powered the Ring Dynasty
His collection almost three hands full
A record pile of jewelry

He caught Page and Reynolds and Raschi and Lopat
Sain and Ford and Turley and
Don Larsen's perfecto
Later he caught Duren and Arroyo
Terry and Stottlemyre and Bouton
Countless counts and calls of strikes and balls
A million squats and blocks and foul tips
And mask adjustments to protect that face

America looking at Yogi
Saw its own reflection
Kids of immigrants could dare to hope
Dare to work their way up

Clad in tools of ignorance
Was no clown, no fool
But a sage man bearing gifts:
Pearls of laughter
Peals of wisdom
Huh?
How seriously to take all this?
Exactly.

HARVEY ON THE MOUND

The outlook wasn't brilliant
        for the Pittsburgh nine that night.
They'd played twelve scoreless with the Braves
        and still no end in sight.
Their pitcher had been perfect,
        setting down all thirty-six
But now was brewing trouble
        and it looked grim for Haddix.

The lead-off Brave got on, you see,
        on the defense's only blunder.
A bunt moved up that tainted man
        and brought up Aaron's thunder.
But Hank was passed, of course,
        to let him swing -- pure folly
So to the plate strode Joe Adcock
        A tough out, too, by golly!

What must have gone through Harvey's head
        as Joe dug in just then?
No doubt a mix of pluck and dread
        if he was like us men.
But that game Harvey on the hill
        stood like a god on Olympus
And with another thunderbolt
        could stop Milwaukee's rumpus.

Thirty-six he had retired
        impeccably and flawless:
Three up, three down times twelve it went,
        the scorebook nearly spotless.
No one had been intact this long;
        no one had ever had to.
No one had ever sung this song;
        let all men ever try to.

Oh, somewhere in this favored land
       the sun is shining bright;
Despite the hit of Adcock
       on that cool spring Tuesday night.
Haddix took his perfect loss
       with perfect class and grace.
Would his gem be half so precious
       had he won that marathon race?

THE DUKE

Edwin D. never woudda made it
Hadda be the Duke of Flatbush
To rule Ebbets

Old smoothie in center
Glided into the ivy and the wood
Brooklyn's All-Star answer
To his ballad companions
Willie and the Mick

Peaked in October
Sure as the leaves outside
But he was a slugger
For all seasons

Duke was delivering
The last of his superb seasons
When I caught up with him
In my rookie year at Forbes
When he smacked one o'er the screen
The nearby barricade in right
Was he already looking ahead
To long lesser seasons in Los Angeles
Or was he already full of nostalgia
For the short porch at home?
His grin as his toe stabbed the plate
Spoke a little of both

Was this man-child of summer
Who threw 300-feet strikes
Ever at home
East coast or west
Or was he all the time waiting
With every slashing swing
And scurrying snatch
For his berth in Cooperstown?

ROBIN

This superhero of Philadelphia
Was hardly in partnership
With the Batman he faced:
Nose as hard as his high one
Roberts helped break the spell --
Twenty win summers about as rare
In the City of Brotherly Love
As a pennant

His was the Whiz
That the kids needed
To go over the top:
Winning at Ebbets
High noon duel with Newk
On the season's final day
Extra effort in extra innings
Liberty Bell pealing for joy

Workhorse of the league
Why go to the pen
With Roberts' sword
Slashing through enemy lineups?

Kept things simple:
Throw strikes, don't let the gophers
Burrow holes in your confidence
Give your team a chance to win
Field your position
Make your swings at bat count
Go for outs and not good impressions
Pitch to win

Springfield rifle arm
Speed exchanged for finesse
Missed the target of 300 wins
But hit the bull's-eye of Cooperstown's Hall --
For Robin Roberts
It was simple

SMOKY

The little round man
From North Carolina
Shake rattle and roll
On the bases
Could wake him up
In the middle of winter
And he'd hit a line drive, they said
Cold off the bench
His manager's southern comfort
In the heat of the pinch

In a pick-up game
You'd probably look at him
And pass, choosing the tall kid
Or the one who ran fastest
Then you'd spend the rest of the day
Regretting he wasn't on your side

Something about him was familiar
He was the shape of your dad or uncle
Had the face of your neighbor
A gas station attendant
With the swing of a lumberjack

When a score of squatting seasons
Took their toll
He became a pure hitter
As naturally as always
Long before the rule
He was designated

Unamuno was right:
Comparisons are odious
But he hit ten points higher than Yogi
Nineteen over Campy, with more hits
And twenty-eight above Johnny, whom he out-tripled
Maybe what keeps him out of Cooperstown
Is that Smoky let his bat do all the talking

EDDIE

Slugger from Texarkana
Joined the Braves in Boston
Left them in Atlanta
In between
Eddie Mathews
Was
Third base for Milwaukee

Fast bat with a swing
Admired by Cobb
Eddie was a rising star
When Boston was flickering out

Kept rising as Milwaukee grew
Into Championship stuff
Eddie and Hank
Became the sport's most potent
One-two punch
Heavyweights that knocked out
Homers by the hundreds

Mathews played under the pressure
Of a man on a pace
After a rookie twenty-five dingers
Followed by nine straight summers
Of thirty or more
What heavier burden than to be
"Ahead of Ruth's pace"?

Eddie in fact was only on pace
To give the game all he had
Happened to be five hundred twelve
But so much more than home runs!

Fiery glove at the hot corner
Fighter every inning on the diamond
Eye for the base on balls
Runs and ribbies always there
Around the century mark

Come October
How fitting that it was Eddie
Who got to pencil in Hank's name
That April day in '74
When the world learned the folly
Of being on pace
And the greatness of living up
To one's own expectations

MR. CUB

"Let's play two!"
Even if Banks never said it
It's the perfect phrase to associate forever
With Ernie

First black in Wrigley's pack
After barnstorming for Cool Papa
Ernie had gifted wrists and a winning smile
Cubbie fans couldn't get enough
Of Ernie in nine
So let's play two today

Sunny days at Wrigley Field
Ernie at short or first
A plus at either position
But oh what a hitter
Those wrists made
Feathery bat waved high
Then slashed like a buggy whip
Balls in the catcher's mitt
Suddenly yanked into the ivy

MVP? Well where would the Cubs be
Without those Banks' shots?
Number 14 on a pennant after Ernie retired
512-mile high peak scaled

Managers had an easy choice
For the heart of their order
Let's play *these* two: Banks and Williams

Ernie so played like a winner
Sure as money in the bank
That we marvel his teams
Never made it to a Series
Bet if they had
Ernie would say when it was over
Let's play two

MICKEY

No mining lead and zinc for Mutt's boy
Gave him a ballplayer's name
Taught him to hit from both sides
Before he could bicycle
Taught him the way out
Taught him The Game

Mickey's lightning legs took him
The rest of the way
Up the alphabet
Beyond Triple-A
To the Stadium

Look up tape-measure home run
Three-point-one to first on the drag bunt
That's Mutt Mantle's kid

Look up World Series
Hall of Fame
That's Mutt's Triple-Crown Mickey

In the sport's genealogy
He descends directly from DiMaggio
But the kid from Oklahoma
Will always be
Mutt's pride of the Yankees
And joy of his heart

SAY HEY

Recall Willie for "The Catch"
His four-dinger day or his 660
Or for a tackle:

His Giants were battling on the road
Sunday's twin bill was crucial
Conditions ripe for basebrawl
Just a matter of time
Till the beanballs drew warnings
Baking dugouts spilled their contents
To converge in a dog fight in the dust

Willie sacked his teammate with the bat
As if to say
Hey, it's a *game*

Willie said the same thing
With every slick basket catch and
Pulled triple over third
He could excite a crowd
With a foul ball

His face lit up the field
Mays played each game
All-Star showcase
And October classics included
As if he were on the other side
Of that wall in center
Out in the streets
The biggest kid in the stickball game
The one who made the game fun
Joy to the world

ROCKY

Wasn't just Somebody up there
Who liked this Rocky from the Bronx
But the whole city of Cleveland:
Love affair with the slugger
Burned brightly for four summers
Ecstasy when the original Rocky IV
Flew out of Baltimore's ring
Cool June night in '58

Rocco Domenico Colavito
The Rock upon which the Indian fans
Built a temple of adoration and hope --
Back grew stronger each season
Surely soon to carry the Tribe back
To October's Game

Threw KO punches with a thundering right
Leaving enemy baserunners
Flat on their sacks
Even threw from the mound a few times
Teasing imaginations as if
The New Bambino was incarnate again

Rocky was the heavyweight to answer
Mickey's bombs and the Killer's jabs
Hero to send the hometown experts
Scrambling for the tape measure

Suddenly the perfect marriage ended
Split up by Trader Frank --
Batting champ with the name
Of an invisible rabbit
Could never take Rocky's place
In Cleveland hearts

Second time around
Seasonal reminders
Of the five missing years
When Rocky's best shots were swung

In Detroit and K.C. trunks --
Too too soon it was over
On the rocks for good
Irreversible
As infatuation

MR. TIGER

Two years and two decades
In the same Detroit uniform
Solid as the concrete and steel
At the corner of Michigan and Trumbull
You bet you can call him Al
Mr. Tiger

Try to look up his roots
In the levels below the majors
You won't find anything
But dented target O's from rocks
Tossed at passing B & O boxcars
Kaline broke in and stayed
At the top

Fame came early for Al
Batting title younger than Cobb
His 200-hit near-MVP soph summer

Can't paint his career by numbers
(Just under 400 homers and .300 or
Just over 3,000 hits in 10,000 tries)
Only with brushstrokes of quiet brilliance
Consistent colors of
Intelligent Gold Glovework by one hand
Smooth and measured as Joe D.
While the other threw cut-down
Bull's-eye darts ahead of runners
Racing but doomed to be the next out

With bold lines of clutch hitting
Shades of Rocky's power
Blended with Harvey's eye
Enough dash to get the job done

With the wonderful gift
For coming back from broken bones
Like an unsinkable warrior

Kaline played the field right
Like a tireless Seurat possessed
To fill the canvas stretched
Between the foul lines
Inning by inning
For two decades and two years
With a masterpiece

HAMMER

Hank assaulted the game's most famous number
The Babe's mystic 714
No one was supposed to be able
To scale that Everest
Surely the air was too thin
The terrain too tricky
And the pressure
Crushing

But 714 was there
The climb had to be made

Destined by his Aa to rank first
Hank seemed to grow stronger each summer
While others slowed and wound down
He climbed on

Destined by his color to rank second
Hank seemed more outspoken each season
While others quietly accepted the rules
He climbed on

Passing all the sacred numbers
Despite the heat of Georgia
Beyond the resting place of Cooperstown
Aaron climbs on yet:
Raising up the Game
With his innings left

ROBERTO

No scorecard necessary
To tell who Number 21 was:

Clemente threw lasers at the bases
Terrorizing enemy baserunners
Or preventing them
With lazy basket-catches
Or streaking stabs
With leaps at the wall
Or dives along the foul line
Habitually converting doubles
To nines in the scorebook
Or reducing them to singles
He was a master of the carom

Roberto ran as no other
Slashing away at the wind
That dared hold him back
From his journey home
Leaving behind his helmet
And caution
Arriba!

Of course his hits
Would total a perfect
Three thousand
Before he was suddenly lost
Post-season:
The time for character
Always his brightest time

Responding to Nicaraguans
In the wake of an earthquake
Clemente stepped onto the plane
From the on-deck circle
Of a life of unorthodox intensity

Roberto played proud
And made proud
His land and race
And the city
So far from where
In the dark of
New Year's Eve
The star fell

HOOT

For most of the sixties
And a few years after
Bob Gibson was
The Cardinal rule

This terrorist was known
Not just for where
He tossed his exploding grenades
(The inside of the plate was his --
Let the crowder beware)
But how:
An old-fashioned arm pump
Then a trademark whirl that
Lifted him
And us

In between heaves
Gibby was all eyes:
They seemed to burn past batters
And focus on the padded backstop
Who was shielded from the glare
And who dare not disturb
The rhythm of the executions

The cool of October's games
Only revved up his heat a notch:
Seven W's in nine tries
Punctuated by scores of clutch K's --
Gibson was at home
Taking the hill for
Game seven

FRANK

Crowded the Game
Like he crowded the plate
Frank Robinson needed no help
Making All Star for Cincinnati:
Premier of the Reds
War was never cold
When Frank was in the battle
Trying to bury you

DeWittingly swapped to Baltimore
After a decade of Crosley bings
Became F. Robbie
On the Oriole express
Triple-crown conductor
To Octobers

Weaver's dream
Along with Boog and Blair
And dynastic duo partner Brooksie
F. stood for four Series tickets
Filling Memorial with memories:
Drop your crab cakes and *watch*
Maybe Frank'll crank *another* one out

F. came to stand for fantastic Four
Behind Hank & Willie & the Babe
Not bad company
For all-time
Frank was always and only comfortable
Batting clean-up

Bi-leagual MVP
On collision course with Cooperstown
Frank played like he had something to prove
So the Game need not have been surprised
At this second Robinson to be a first:
Robinson *managed* somehow
To make his point

Saw Robbie crush one at old Forbes
Swear it nicked the shortstop's glove
Rising like a golf ball
Up and over the bricks
Not a majestic trajectory
But a solid working-man's swing
Got the job done

SANDY

Crowd into the stadium
On the day Koufax was throwing
And enjoy the anticipation

Keep your eye on the ball
While he lobs his first warmups
Pretty soon it will be just a blur
Something in the vicinity of
The opposition swings
Rumored to be solid

Get set to fill your scorecard
With K's -- some twisted around
Like the fanning batters
Start counting --
Double-digits in whiffs today?

Probably not too many runs on deck
The Dodgers will scratch for their few
Maybe one will be enough --
After all, Sandy's on the mound

If he's *really* on
Then watch out --
Anything can happen
How long since his *last* no-no?
What would today's make it?

Sandy's career was
Six years of wrestling for control
And a half dozen of being there
Being on top of his profession
Glowing in the Octobers
He earned for his team
A nova increasingly brilliant
Then suddenly gone

Sandy was still just thirty
So much was ahead
How many more shutouts
Southpaw strikeouts
And low-hit gems?
Come to the stadium still
Scan the leagues
For fire-ballers who dream of being
The next Koufax

MAZ

Coal-miner's son
Wizard
Of his seasons
Object of awe
From fellow all-stars
His small tattered glove
Ripened into gold

His stats dazzle
Far less
Than his craft
Yet they glow
Mightily

Pirate pitchers in trouble
And fans alike
Prayed aloud
For deliverance from a rally:
Hit it to Maz

Master of the
Six-four-three cascade
Artist of the forces:
Four-six and four-three
Balladeer of the saving
Two!
Maker of mystic DPs
Fabled POs and As --
The uncommon Es
Only served as reminders
That he was of this world
After all

Might as well recall Ruth
Strictly for his fielding
As believe Maz can be summed
In that infamous
Clout

HONDO

Giant who was not so gentle
With his club
Broke into the NL big
As if descended from a beanstalk
With no Jack to save the pitchers

Dealt to the Senators
He then dealt capital punishment
To the other league
Resembling in one '68 burst
No one as much as Joe Hardy
Come from the midwest
To slay the Yankees:
Ten dingers in twenty trips!
Must be an Applegate in the stands
To credit with an assist!
That was the week that *was*

But this Atlas could not alone
Lift the D.C. comics
Into the Series

Remember Frank Howard
For his summer power drills
Dueling with the Killer
Yaz and Reggie
For the HR crown

Made the bat looked small
Then the ball
As it soared:
Look! Up in the sky!
Superman's connected!

We can only wonder
What might have happened
Had the splendid Splinter
Gotten into Hondo's eye sooner

Strongman folk-hero
Thrilled the home crowds:
Homer off Whitey in Game 4
Of the Los Angeles sweep in '63
All-Star dinger in '69
In Washington
Not the only cities which
In the Sixties
Needed something solid

BROOKSIE

Man from Arkansas
More than a Little Rock at third
Brooks Robinson anchored the Orioles
For nearly a quarter century

Sure as fireworks on the Fourth
Were his spectacular feats
At the hot corner

Brooks prospected his gold
With ambidexterity
Panning along the line
Guarding his claim to fortune
Diving for white nuggets
Following his instincts
In the hole at short
And blasting his finds to basemen
Cutting down the enemy's rush

Offense was overshadowed dessert
Leather was his meat and potatoes
Charging bunts or toppers
Knocking down thunder
Then whirling sidearm heat

B. Robbie not just stole the spotlight
His sideshow became center stage
Box seats along third
Choice of the stadium
Watch the performer up close
Impossible to distract
His shining confidence

Like an old Oriole
Brooks hung in there
Until finally spiked high
By time
Veins tapped out
Robinson left behind

A new gold standard
(Nettles "Robinsonian" in '78,
Glittering A-5s "Brooksian"
From then on)
And memories of Octobers
Touched by his Midas glove

THE DOMINICAN DANDY

If it's Opening Day
And in the sixties
(Calendar and thermometer)
Then the odds are good that
Juan Marichal will be out there
Making the Giants 1-0

San Francisco workhorse
Durable dominance personified
Pitched more All-Star innings
Than post-season

Zeroes were his thing:
Zipped the H column once
Blanked R in fifty-one others
Including one string of
Sixteen pearls against Spahnie

Juan kicked higher, showing the batter
The twenty-seven on his back
And the corners of the plate
But not the ball:
That was a cloud of white
Fog in a low twisting jet stream
Moving from point P to point K

Marichal's remarkable right arm:
Torch of Candlestick
Beacon on the path to October
Frisco's answer to Koufax and Gibson
Limb dips low
As the left foot spikes sky
A counterbalance
As if suspended on tightrope
Poised and ready
To whirl from tangled angles
When foot inevitably plunges
Earthward

Had he pitched later
In the other league
Where pitchers are spared
The chore of handling the bat
Juan's career might have gone
Unblemished
On the other hand
In the sixties it was not easy
To admit mistakes
To forgive and move on --
Giant steps forward then and now

BILLY

Gonna sit right down
And write myself a ballplayer:
Gonna have a swing oh so sweet
Injury-proof arms and feet
Work his way up from the bottom
Chicago will be glad they got him:
Billy Williams
Oh yeah

Mechanical man of the sixties
Cub outfielder was
Consistency personified:
Mass-produced summers
Of twenty-plus homers
Eighty-plus ribbies
Gilded in .290 shades of gold
Special-delivered to Cub fans
With a quiet tip of the cap

Whistler's (Ala.) son
Middle name of a lion
As Wrigley as the field's ivy
Billy Williams was a powerful
Six hundred ABs a season
Statement:
Sure as the mail must go through
Williams will be in the lineup
Swinging elegance
Oh yeah

STRETCH

The rookie
The Other Willie
Burst into headlines in '59
Like the Hurricane that crushed the NL
Two years earlier in Milwaukee down the
Stretch

McCovey after Cepeda!
Giant footsteps to follow
Had to play first base sooner or later
With a stretch
Like Willie's

Took some time before he became a regular
On the honor roll
Beside his a-Mays-ing teammate
For slugging homers and ribbies

The AL had Mantle and Maris
But the San Francisco M & M Boys
The Alabama Willies
(Not to mention Juan M more)
Had muscle with staying power
Their swirling sticks
Stretching over thirteen windy summers

Willie McCovey's career
Stretched over four different decades
And is as jammed with highlight hits
As an inning stuffed with two homers (twice)
Or an upper deck packed with fans
Imagining a tape measure
S t r e t c h e d
From home plate to their hands
No matter how far away they sat

Despite the five hundred and dozen dingers
Clustered along his evolutionary line
Between pheenom and bronze plaque --

McCovey's best-remembered swing
Came at the end of his only Series
And Willie would have been the hero
If only his two-on two-out liner
Had somehow eluded Bobby Richardson's
Stretch

SIXTY-NINE

Mounds were lowered to half-mast
Because hitting had died.
Men walked on the moon.
Curt Flood walked to Court.
Leagues halved into divisions
And the Cubs salivated:
Pennant scent stronger than beer
In bleachers sagging with rookie bums.

Chicago cheerleaders joined
By the third-sacker
With the Golden Glove:
Ronald Edward Santo from Seattle.

Ron couldn't have remembered the last flag
Hoisted at Wrigley:
Jolly Cholly's second turn at the helm,
Cavaretta's .355 and Wyse's 22 W's,
In the war-thinned drive of '45.

Down the stretch
While Leo bit his lip,
While Ernie and Billy and Jim and Randy
Littered the crowds of thirty-something thousand
With souvenirs of the pursuit,
Ron Santo's choleric charisma
Drove in runs -- one-two-three.

Santo clicked his heels after victories at home
Like a rain-maker determined to end a drought
Until nice guy Hodges finished first
Ending the dream instead.

In the stretches of desert
Between October oases,
We remember best
Those who offer rare cool sips
Tasting of yesterdays and tomorrows
And those who celebrate,

As we will when we arrive,
Even if they only saw
What turned out to be
Unforgettable mirage.

Can't pry sixty-nine away
From Cub fans:
Like a Santo-sent shot
Bound for glory
With the wind at its back
And caught on the fly --
It's a keeper.

WILLIE

Like fine wine
This Willie seemed to get better
With age
And wiser

Wilver Dornel Stargell
Broke into Pirate yearbooks
As a skinny Oklahoman labeled
Pittsburgh Pirate Possibility
Eyes full of "I think I can"
Left the city to the sound of
Pops of champagne
Cover story on a
Hall of Fame program
Smile shouting "I knew I could"

In between
Willie's two decades of play
Created a windmill full of memories:
Blasts up on the roof at Forbes
Third deck at Three Rivers and Busch
Over the bleachers in L.A.
Stargell was a longer version
Of another Willie's motto:
Hit 'em where *nothing* ain't

Caught Roberto's royal touch
Caught teammates doing things right
Rewarding them with gold stars:
Every employee's fantasy

Black native American power
Star to gel a team together
Foreman of the Lumber Company
Good provider of Chicken on the Hill
Willie left the game right:
October talent show
Fall fireworks lighting up

Starry nights and shining back
Over star-spangled
Banner summers:
Tip of the cap --
Applause
Still echoing

PETE ROSE

To be or not to be
Admitted to the Hall:
That's the hot stove question
Fueling our coming to grips
With what the Hall is
And is not

It is not a pantheon
And though we pilgrimage there
We dare not worship

The Hall is still but a place
That recalls and honors great deeds
And their doers
And while we remember
Admire with awe
And gain inspiration,

We must concede
That those honored
Simply played exceedingly well
An all too human game

Let he who is without
Cast the first
Ballot without
The old Red Rose:
So ruled the slain umpire

In the interim or forever
Fate has chosen the
Most fitting punishment
For this hitter:

Condemned to the on-deck circle
Rolling like Sisyphus
His stone of lost innocence
Up the Cooperstown slope
Only to see it heaved back down
By cowardly gods
Knowing not themselves
Nor what they defend

FERGIE

Five times he suitcased to a new team
But he's stuck in time
As the Cubbie ace --
Six straight summers
Of scoring a score of successes --
Ferguson Jenkins
Gave Leo no lip
When turned out of the pen

Never had the chance to show his stuff
To the world in a Series
Fergie All Star showcased only twice:
Hubbelling six K's his first 20 season
Back again in his Cy Young year

Jenkins was a great Canadian
Without the support of a great Club:
Durable and enduring:
Forty-five shutouts on the *wrong* end
Seasons of coming close

Three-thousand-some strikeouts
Spangled over a fluorescent career
Lit the path to the Hall
Bronze was his
Like the plate was his
When Fergie took the hill

LITTLE JOE

Bonanza for the Reds
In a multi-horse swap with Houston
This Little Joe helped make
Cincinnati's Machine
Bigger and better

Texan was hardly a lone star
In Red Riverfront Valley:
So the name Morgan
Is strung up today
With Bench and Rose and Perez
Griffey and Foster and Concepcion --
Latter-day Murderer's Row
Armed for shootouts at any corral
Likely to come out more than O.K.

Joe Morgan grew like a tall tale
Each summer embellishing skills:
Sharp-shooter's eye
Glove to keep his turf saddle soap clean
Quick-draw speed on the bases

Wasn't a chicken wing flapping
When Little Joe was at bat
But a deadly timing device
Cocking for pistol shots
Or dynamite blasts
Seemingly out of proportion
With his size and weight

No idle threat
Joe bandited bases regularly
Striking terror into enemy batteries
Rattling infielders
Stealing the show

Durable second-sacker
Good for the long hauls:
Traffic-directing field general in

Pennant runs down September stretches
Morgan made it to seven post-seasons
Four Series rings to sport

Joe always seemed to get what he wanted
Clutch hits or steals --
Cooperstown:
Who would be surprised
If he made the Hall all over again
In the company of mikemen?

TOM TERRIFIC

Latter-day Mathewson
Kid from California
Might have won as many
But as fate would have it
Tom Seaver on the mound
Was surrounded by Mets

Core of the Big Apple team
Put the W in New
And the K in York
Put the Mets in the Series
Loveable losers learned
Not just how to play the game
But how to follow a leader
To October

We know he pitched for other teams
But it seems like he won all 311
With that first franchise

"Fast" ball an understatement
We know that if K's were hung
Along Shea's upper deck
For all his strikeouts
The stadium would sag
But it seems like we remember
Tom Terrific
More for his intelligent
Selections and quotations
Than his artful velocity

Seaver caused the maniac fans
To drown out the passing jets
When he set up shop
And started grinding that right knee
Into the dirt

Easier to wash those stains
From the uniform
Bearing number Forty-One
Than to lose the memories
Of this grand competitor --
But who would want to?

MR. OCTOBER

Straw stirred a lot of
Troubled waters in his time

Uniforms changed
But not Reggie Jackson
He showed through them all
Oozing with showman's confidence

Reggie gave us so much more
Than a candy bar:
Photographs galore captioned
With heroic words;
Memories aplenty
Of tremendous swings
Bashes off All Star roof lights
Enough power connections
So that the record K's
Are all but forgotten

Earned his autumnal nickname
Because that's where this driver
Parked his teams: October's Game

Was this soul man of swat
A natural wonder of power
Like Niagara Falls
Or a man-made tower of strength
Like the pyramids?

Preferred Reggie-ball to Billy
Jackson swaggered all the way
Especially those trademark trots
When the ball was launched
Somewhere across the sea
Of white shirts in the bleachers
And his style went on parade

Saw him once wearing pinstripes
Grinning while the Fenway faithful
Did their best to deflate his
Summer wind --
Hit or miss
Reggie's excess at the bat
In calm dissonance with the hostile noise
Was worth the price of admission

JOHNNY

If Bench had been around
When they were nicknaming the equipment
Stuff might today be known as
The Tools of Dominance

Johnny was the driver
Of the Big Red Machine
Steered it unswerving to October's Game
All during the Seventies --
Cranked it alive with his bat
Horsepower to spare
Kept it shiny with his golden mitt
Pushed it home when it needed gas
Till his legs finally gave out

Behind the plate
Bench showed his pitchers one hand
Saved the other for rifle throws to the bags --
Bench mark left on the position
Indicates how he elevated it for all to survey

Cleanup man did his job
With consistency and style
No backstop slammed more homers
Rookie of the Year
Only the first of many awards
Two-time MVP collected
All along the way to the Hall

Like Yogi of the Yanks
J. B. became a symbol
Pride of Cincinnati
Playing hard in post-season glare
Standing firm and blocking
Anything less than best effort
Making the sure-handed tag on fame
With dignity and distinction
Gave to the game a touch of his class

JIM

Swing as compact as his name
Jim Rice
Was wrists strong enough
To snap a bat
On a checked swing

Heir to the spot held by Ted and Yaz
In left
In the lineup
In the hearts of Bosox fans

Rice arrived in seventy-five
With a kid named Fred:
Righty-lefty rookie tandem
Led Boston to October's Game --
Broken bone, broken heart finish

Consistent hit man with power:
Only Jim Rice ever strung together
Three straight sparkling summers
Of two hundred hits
Thirty-five-plus dingers

Jim bruised the Green Monster
Black and blue
With his rocket shots

Jim played the Green Monster
Decoy and carom
With his rocket throws

Played tall, like that Wall
Spoke more by just being there
Something that wouldn't go away
Sooner or later
Had to recognize it
Deal with it
Respect it

YOU KNOW ME, DON'T YOU?

I am baseball. I've looked pretty much the same for over a hundred summers. That sounds like I'm old, but I *feel* young.

Find me in the eyes of a Little Leaguer, or those of kids out with the ballpark crowd for the first time. Some say I look best in sunlight, on grass, on a Sunday in July. But that's me, even on a cold April night, even inside a dome.

Don't make the mistake of confusing me with those who play the game. Baseball is not greedy, nor am I skinflint owners or TV folk who sell commercials. Players may auction themselves off, bet on or throw games, and shun the fans. They may be ignorant about my past. They may even think they are baseball, but they are not.

Look past them all. See me in the turning of a 6-4-3 double play and a rookie's first hit. See me in the sweat on the forehead of the pitcher straining for the last out. See me in the autograph easily signed with a smile, the tip of the cap, the glance toward the stands when in a pinch. See me in the moment when suddenly everybody stands to see where the long ball will land.

I knew your grandfather when he could hardly speak English, but spoke baseball fluently with his neighbors. I knew your father when he was given his first glove, when he played in the street and in vacant lots, from morning till dusk. And I'm getting to know your son, who puts on his team's catcher's gear like it's a suit of armor.

Don't you recognize my voice? It's in the buzz of the fans that you hear on the radio, and the crack of the bat. It's vendors hawking peanuts and sodas, kids squealing on a playground, Moms and Dads rooting for their kids to get a hit.

I was there long before the Black Sox, and I'm still here. I was there before Jackie Robinson, in every league in the land, and I'm still here. I was there before radio and television, before Curt Flood, before the big money, and I'm still here. Tough as horsehide standing its ground against swinging wood, I am baseball, and will be here as long as people let me into their lives.

You know me now, don't you? *I am baseball*, the summer game, alive, sturdy as a family tree.

ABOUT THE AUTHOR

Gene Carney is a native of Pittsburgh, but he has now spent more years in upstate New York. Gene and his wife Barbara have two grown children and one terrific marriage. A former social worker, Gene now writes and edits full-time. His book *Burying the Black Sox: How Baseball's Cover-Up of the 1919 World Series Fix Almost Succeeded* (Potomac Books, 2006) won SABR's Larry Ritter Award. Gene has also written numerous short stories, articles, reviews, humor, a novella, and a full-length play (now a musical) – all baseball. *A Baseball Family Album* is his second collection of baseball poetry.

www.ingramcontent.com/pod-product-compliance
Lightning Source LLC
LaVergne TN
LVHW051832080426
835512LV00018B/2829